A Dirty Guide to
a Clean Home

A Dirty Guide to a Clean Home

Housekeeping Hacks You Can't Live Without

MELISSA DILKES PATERAS

The Laundry Lesbian you've seen on TikTok

with Carla Sosenko

THE DIAL PRESS • NEW YORK

This is a work of nonfiction. Some names
and identifying details have been changed.

Copyright © 2023 by Melissa Dilkes Pateras

Illustrations copyright © 2023 by Alexis Seabrook

All rights reserved.

Published in the United States by The Dial Press,
an imprint of Random House, a division of
Penguin Random House LLC, New York.

THE DIAL PRESS is a registered trademark
and the colophon is a trademark of
Penguin Random House LLC.

LIBRARY OF CONGRESS CATALOGING-IN-PUBLICATION DATA

NAMES: Pateras, Melissa Dilkes, author. | Sosenko, Carla.

TITLE: A dirty guide to a clean home: housekeeping hacks
you can't live without / Melissa Dilkes Pateras with Carla Sosenko.

DESCRIPTION: First edition. | New York: The Dial Press, [2024]

IDENTIFIERS: LCCN 2023012779 (print) | LCCN 2023012780 (ebook) |
ISBN 9780593446379 (hardcover) | ISBN 9780593446386 (ebook)

SUBJECTS: LCSH: House cleaning. | Housekeeping.

CLASSIFICATION: LCC TX324.P375 2024 (print) |
LCC TX324 (ebook) | DDC 648/.5—dc23/eng/20230331

LC record available at https://lccn.loc.gov/2023012779

LC ebook record available at https://lccn.loc.gov/2023012780

Printed in the United States of America on acid-free paper

randomhousebooks.com

2 4 6 8 9 7 5 3 1

FIRST EDITION

Book design by Barbara M. Bachman

*To my children whom I love
with every ounce of my being—
Morgan, Noah, and Aidan,
you know which one of you is my favorite.*

*To my beautiful Trace who I met
on a dancing app for children.
I love you more than coffee
but please don't make me prove it.*

CONTENTS

3.

This Is Where You
Look After the Machines You
Spent So Much Money On

The Birth of
THE LAUNDRY LESBIAN

. . .

Y OU KNOW THOSE SIGNS SOME PEOPLE HAVE HANGING IN THEIR homes? The ones that say things like, "Live, Laugh, Love," or "Home Is Where the Heart Is?" Perhaps you're someone who has one, or more, of those signs. No disrespect. Home *is* where the heart is. I, too, want to live, laugh, love. But the one sign I take issue with—and if it's hanging in your home, I apologize in advance—is the one that says, "Please excuse the mess, we're making memories."

I hate that sign.

It's the worst quote ever, "Please excuse the mess, we're making memories." No, you aren't—at least not good ones. You're living in chaos and *those* are the memories you are making. I hate the idea that you can't be making memories while also keeping a neat home, be-

cause you *can*. In fact, I think you can make even better memories—
with less stress, anxiety, and worry—in a tidy home.

To me, a kept house is a form of anxiety relief and self-care, an
adult life skill that makes me feel good about living in my home; a
place I don't dread coming home to at the end of the day and instead
am proud to invite others into; a place to feel comfortable and safe.

If your house is in disarray, it can be hard to know how you got
here—surely, your house wasn't always such a mess?! A messy home
can be paralyzing. You might even feel panic-stricken about the pros-
pect of tidying up, or ashamed when someone pops by unexpectedly.
You are not alone in feeling like the task is insurmountable; a lot of
people feel this way. Imagine for a minute you are pushing a shopping
cart filled with bags of cement up a steep hill, on a rainy day, wearing
Crocs you swore you would NEVER leave the house in. This is what
adulting can feel like, and maybe no one ever prepared you for it. *Is
there a secret? Why do I feel like I'm not in the know?* you may wonder—
some people make it look so easy. *Did I miss the memo? Why don't they
teach this in school?* Worry no longer: I am here to prepare you, tell you
there *is* a secret. I'll make sure you're soon in the know, and this book
is the memo. The key is hitting reset and approaching housekeeping
from a different, less overwhelming, piece-by-piece sort of way. Believe it or not, a home can create a sense of self-esteem, pride, and
calm—and *anyone* can have that. Even you. Which means you can
make memories *minus* the mess.

You may have bought this book because you follow me on TikTok,
where you know me as The Laundry Lesbian. Maybe you picked it up
at the bookstore and wondered why someone who looks like me knows
anything about cleaning or laundry; or maybe someone gifted it to you
and you're thinking, *Hang on a minute, what are they trying to tell me?*
It's not every day that a heavily tattooed, middle-aged lesbian mother
of three is presented as a lifestyle guru. But here I am, the voice of
authority behind the book you're holding in your hands right now. I
gained a large following on TikTok in 2020 because I folded a fitted
sheet to soothing music with a wink and a pat and then patched a hole
in my wall while making as many jokes as possible about my enormous
caulk. Who knew that so many people would be interested in tips and

tricks around the home while laughing at my juvenile jokes? But what has surprised me the most is how many people were genuinely hungry for the information. A frequent comment on my TikToks has been, "What is this sorcery?" which always makes me laugh because it implies that I am somehow performing magic tricks. To me, housekeeping isn't magic, it's just something I was taught. I'm not a gatekeeper. I want to break the magician's oath and let the secret out.

I was seeing TikTok after TikTok with questions directed to me, things like, "How do I remove this stain?" Or, "What's the best way to fold a towel?" One woman's post really struck an emotional chord for me. Her TikTok was about how she grew up in a disorganized, dirty house and her parents were hoarders. She wanted to break the cycle but didn't know how. Living in that environment, she had never been taught, at home or at school. And here she was turning to TikTok for advice. That's not the part that made me emotional—asking for help is a brave thing. What made me emotional was the shame that came along with not knowing these things (how to organize a closet, keep your whites white, repair your dishwasher) that adults were "supposed" to know.

This was one of many stories that made me resolve to help people see that housework isn't sorcery; there's no need for shame, and successful adulting *is* an attainable goal. So maybe you're a fan wanting more, maybe you were right to purchase this book at the bookstore, or maybe someone gifted it to you not because they wanted to offend you but because they wanted to help you. I know that the tips and techniques in these pages will be useful, transformative even, for all of you. I hope this can be the most helpful book you've ever read.

So how did I get here? How did I learn everything I know? Let me tell you about who I learned most of it from: Her name was Gladys. She was my grandmother, and I affectionately called her Nan. My nan was the one who inspired my passion for housework and home maintenance. Let me paint you a picture of Nan. She worked full-time for Hallmark Cards. And this was back in the day where she was on a production line making cards by hand. You've never seen anyone with as many paper cuts on her hands as my nan. She was allowed to take home two cards a week, which she organized in boxes, always ready with a card for any occasion, birthday, wedding, get well, Hanukkah—even though she didn't know anyone Jewish, she was ready.

As a kid I spent a lot of time at Nan's house. I would watch her strategically move through the house on a very tight cleaning schedule. That woman was very task oriented. Each day would be designated to a specific chore: Mondays was dusting, Tuesday was floors. And these tasks were just in addition to her everyday keep-ups. The bed was made the second she got up, the bathroom got a once-over right after she bathed, dishes were washed immediately after each meal. She was a tidy-and-clean-as-you-go kind of woman who did her daily tasks on *top* of the deep cleaning. She was organized, structured, and resourceful; nothing went to waste, everything had a secondary use (she'd even use my grandpa's old undies as rags). And there I was, little rough-and-tumble BMX bandit Melissa, completely in awe of this domestic superhero. I didn't realize the valuable lessons I was taking in just by watching her.

Nan did everything herself: She cooked, cleaned, grew her own vegetables, painted the house, and wrapped presents with the most amazing embellishments before that was even a thing. Her house was always stocked with food which she bought from seven different grocery stores in order to get the best deal. She sewed, repaired things, made her own cleaning products, all while saving money and being efficient. This is a woman who didn't have many modern conveniences: She didn't have a dishwasher, a modern washing machine, or a dryer. She scrubbed stains out of clothes on a washboard and put them through a wringer and hung them to dry and then ironed everything. She had tips and tricks for everything to do with cleaning. I picked things up along the way because I loved spending time with her. She made me feel safe and the routine of cleaning and organizing helped calm my chaotic brain. I am grateful to have had her as a role model; not everyone is as fortunate. Looking back at it now, I'm doubtful she would have any idea that this was the birth of The Laundry Lesbian.

The other crucial part of the alchemy that made me the self-reliant rebel that I am was necessity: My sisters are seven and nine years older than me, so it's fairly clear that I may have been the result of a party my parents had in August of 1974. Without my wonderful parents having tired of parenting by the time I came along, I would never have benefited from their free-range parenting style. I wouldn't be the creative, resourceful, confident, fix-it machine that I am.

AS MUCH AS I loved my nan, I'm not her and this book isn't about me trying to convince you to be her. If it were, it would be called *Project Nan: How to Be My Nan in 1,001 Easy Steps*. But what my nan did for me is what I want to pass on to you. All the building blocks of what she taught me are still here, but I've found a way to adapt them into my life in a way that works for me. In the same way that an apple a day keeps the doctor away, I believe that a little clean and tidy every day keeps the housework at bay. I am the least likely character in this story. I'm not naturally gifted in this area—in fact, there are a lot of reasons I'm not a natural fit for domestic inclination: I have a severe attention-deficit hyperactivity disorder.

———

. . . SORRY, I SAW SOMETHING SHINY, WHERE WERE WE? AH
yes, my difficulty with focusing. Like I was saying, my brain isn't on
cruise control; it always wants to detour. I have a hard time focusing
and staying on task, but with a little help from Nan I have managed
to develop systems and stick with them. And if I can do that, believe
me, you can, too.

I am not a professional cleaner, a laundress by trade, or a general
contractor. I did not intern with Marie Kondo, Martha Stewart, or
Bob Vila. I was just a kid who was lucky enough to have my nan to
shape and guide me. ADHD doesn't define me, it's just what I have.
Who I am is a full-time social worker, mom of three, wife, Canadian,
and a lot of other things, just like you are. I don't have a special housekeeping gene or skill set that you don't. My point is that not even I,
who has an entire book on how to take care of your home, am perfect.
I have not mastered life and I can't teach you how to do that either.
But I *can* teach you how to master this one small corner of it: your
home. I've learned a lot along the way and I've realized that having a
system in place is crucial and allows me to keep up instead of having
to catch up. That's something you'll hear me say a lot in this book: If
you keep up, you won't have to catch up—and it's the catching up
that's the overwhelming part. What I'm saying is, adulting doesn't
have to suck. It can be tolerable, rewarding, and *easy*. (I hesitate to say
fun, but you never know.)

My book will move you through the different parts of your home
and the care required to keep you feeling comfortable in and proud of
your space. You can read it cover to cover or dip in and out to use just
the parts that work for you. Think of it like a home-improvement buffet where you can take what you want and leave what you don't.

If you struggle to fold fitted sheets, I'll teach you. If your white
T-shirts are pink because no one ever explained how to do laundry,

allow me. If your closet feels like a wild jungle you'd rather close the doors on than attempt to clean out, fear no more. If you are living with a sense of embarrassment because you don't know where to begin when it comes to making your house tidy—maybe you grew up with messy parents and nobody ever showed you how to clean—I am here to set you off on your journey, absolutely no judgment included.

It's okay not to know how to do things—why would you if you were never taught? There's no shame in that. *A Dirty Guide to a Clean Home* will show you how to do things easily and affordably, with a few innuendos along the way. You may even enjoy it. Because, yes, while chores are, by definition, chores, they don't have to be overwhelming or life-consuming. They can be life-improving!

There is no shame in your housework game, no matter what level you're starting at. That is the entire point of this book. Being neat and tidy doesn't make you a better person, so the opposite (*not* being neat and tidy) doesn't make you a bad one. I am not here to judge you. I am here only to help. If you bought my book, that tells me you want help. If you come to any parts where you're like, "Eff this, I can't do it," simply turn the page and move on. Remember you're at a buffet: Take what works for you, leave what doesn't; this book will always be here for you.

My easy-to-follow instructions will help you feel more confident about housework and maybe even help you enjoy it. Imagine: having a system for laundry that's continuously moving and never building up, so you don't end up with piles everywhere. Or saving a few hundred bucks next time one of the kids accidentally busts a hole in the wall because you (yes, you!) can patch it yourself.

BELIEVE IT OR NOT we are all creatures of habit. Every one of us thrives on structure and routine, no matter what that routine is. We might not want to admit it, but we feel most comfortable on autopilot. This is why most of us don't like change, even if that change is in our best interest. A prime example of when my routine went flying out the window—and I'm sure many of you reading this can relate—was COVID. I didn't even realize how important my routine was until it was gone. Sure, the first week was fun: We reflected on our lives, we planned on baking bread, getting fit, learning a new language or instrument, spending time as a family. But when the novelty wore off and the fear of *How long is this going to last?* set in, suddenly things got real out of hand, fast. My routine was nowhere to be found. Unexpectedly, the entire household was home, 24/7; everyone was fighting for a quiet space to work or study. Suddenly I'd also become a teacher trying to relearn long division to teach my third grader in between my own Zoom meetings, longing for the commute to work that I once dreaded so I could have some alone time. A pandemic side effect for my kids was them constantly confusing boredom with hunger, meaning they needed a meal every hour. Even the pets seemed confused about what was going on. Here we were drowning in chaos and all the while the mess was accumulating around us. We found ourselves wanting our routine back because it was predictable and comfortable. And so we made a point to get back there.

Change is hard. It feels like more work, more effort, and it requires more time and planning. I acknowledge that changing your habits is more work on the front end, but once new systems are in place, a new routine will just be *your* routine—one that works for you and that will become second nature and easier in the long run. So, let's get into the nitty-gritty of this book and by the end, I promise you, it'll be worth it . . . and I'll try my best to keep you laughing along the way.

A Dirty Guide to
a Clean Home

1.

This Is Where
You Get Down
and Dirty

ORGANIZING

This Is Where You Organize Your Mind and All of the Shit You Have Accumulated

. . .

KNOW WHAT YOU'RE THINKING: SHOULDN'T ORGANIZING come *after* cleaning? (It's totally okay if you weren't thinking that. But now that I've mentioned it, you're thinking it, right?) Here's the thing: The more organized you are, the easier it will be to clean and keep things clean. For anyone not naturally inclined toward neatness, the idea of getting organized, let alone *staying* organized, is overwhelming enough. But it's the key to getting a truly clean house, and I have a feeling you might already be more organizationally inclined than you think.

Let's start in your kitchen. If I asked you to think about where you would find your cutlery, I'm willing to bet that it's in an organizer, separated into forks, knives, and spoons. This is the perfect example of a simple organization system that you are already using, and you don't even know you're doing it. What I'm getting at is that you already *do* have areas in your house that have a sense of order to them, where you have a system of what goes where, and that means you have the capacity to extend that organizational skill set elsewhere—even everywhere! It might feel like a lot to think about getting everything into its right place, but even if the only place you're organized is where you keep your forks, you're already doing it a little bit. I bet you have proof of your abilities all around you.

If I asked you to locate any item in your home, wouldn't it be great if you could find it with ease? Imagine having a home for all those pens you "didn't steal" from work or being able to find a safety pin when you need one last-minute. Imagine being able to find the spare batteries you're sure you have somewhere instead of borrowing them from your remote or digging through the junk drawer. You know the

one, we all have one: It's where you have to push past the old take-out menus, past all the electronic cords you have no idea what they're for but you can't throw them away 'cause one day you might find out what mystery device they charge, past the spare piece of paper with someone's number on it and you can't remember who it is but you might need it someday, the free toothbrush you got from the dentist, a three-year-old ChapStick, to maybe, just maybe, find a battery, but it's a AA when you needed a AAA. All that work and now you've disturbed the ecosystem of the drawer—so much that now you can't get the damn thing closed.

I know what you're thinking: Didn't she just say that if I know where to find something, it's organized, at least a little? It's true, I did. But here's the thing about that drawer: When you find a battery, does it always work? Or is it an old one that's out of juice that for some reason you chucked back in there instead of the trash? There is a fine line between having an organizational system that works for you and having a messy dumpster fire of a drawer. Beware of that line.

When it comes to tools to get organized, the list of things you absolutely need is pretty short:

TOOLBOX

- Garbage bags
- Storage
- Labels (optional)
- A gallon of determination
- A shit-ton of focus
- Some time

THIS IS HOW WE DO IT

(I hope you're singing this, not just reading it.)

Start Small and Live Large

I'll tell you what we're not going to do. We're not going to organize your entire home all at once. That's unrealistic, overwhelming, and definitely not how I roll. We are going to start small. Our first goal is to pick a section: one room, one cupboard, one shelf, or even one tiny little drawer. I've said it before and I'll say it again, start small. My aim is to set you up to succeed. As we're just starting out on this organizational journey, I don't want to overwhelm you.

Once you conquer your first small goal, it will give you a sense of accomplishment that will prove to you that you can do this. It will also allow you to move at a pace that works for you. If I asked you to organize one drawer in your kitchen, that would seem like a doable task; but if I asked you to reorganize your entire kitchen, you'd probably get an overwhelming tightness in your chest. If we break it down, section by section, one drawer turns into two, then three, then a shelf, then a cupboard, and before you know it, the kitchen is done, no need for the overwhelming tight feeling in your chest.

When setting a goal, you want to make it SMART! You're a smart cookie, so make your goal SMART, too.

S—Specific: What do I want to accomplish? Target a particular area for improvement.

M—Measurable: How will I know when it is accomplished?

A—Achievable: How will the goal be accomplished? Is it actually possible to achieve it?

R—Realistic: Can you feasibly achieve your goals using the available resources?

T—Timebound: When do you want to achieve this by?

Let's break down SMART goals so they're not so boring-presentation-at-a-work-conference:

- Specific: Pick one section of your home to organize. Start with a small drawer, a small shelf, that top cupboard, or perhaps, if you're feeling adventurous, your entire closet. Whatever the section, be detailed and clear about what you want to accomplish and stick to it.
- Measurable: Let's stick with the drawer example: It's a small space, so it'll be easy to know when you're finished. Once everything in it is easy to access and find, meaning no more shuffling the mess around just to get the damn thing closed, stay on track.
- Achievable: Make sure the space you choose to organize is achievable. If the thought of cleaning out your closet all at once makes you feel overwhelmed, then pick something smaller, perhaps just your T-shirts. That's more achievable. Make sure you are in the right mood to tackle the section you have picked. The more you achieve, the more motivation you'll have to keep the ball rolling (and you know I love balls).
- Realistic: Ask yourself, *Do I have all the tools I need to complete this project?* If it's a drawer, maybe you need a drawer organizer; if it's a closet, maybe you need shoe boxes; if it's the dreaded Christmas decorations in the basement, maybe you need storage bins. Whatever the section, make sure you have the necessary tools needed on hand and ready to go before you start. You don't want to have to stop halfway through to go to the store to

get the items you need, run into Brenda while you're there, end up having a thirty-minute catch-up about how the kids are doing and then suddenly realize you need to get home and make dinner and no longer have time to finish the task at hand.

- Timebound: This is the big one, the real cause of our anxiety, because it's something we never feel we have enough of. Make sure you set aside the time to start and finish the task. This means, be strict and give yourself a deadline. If anyone knows distraction it's me, so if you only have an hour, perhaps today is not the day to do the entirety of your closet. You don't want to have to stop halfway through because you have to pick your kid up from basketball practice and then come home and help your other kid with their science project that you just found out is due tomorrow. So perhaps an hour is best set aside for a drawer, or if you're feeling courageous, perhaps two drawers. Make the time that fits the space you want to tackle, pop on some tunes, and get it done.

Abide by the Keep, Toss, Donate, Sell Rule

The best approach to a real declutter-and-organize is to remove all the items from that space and divide them into four piles/categories:

1. Things to keep
2. Things to throw away
3. Things to donate
4. Things to sell (Yes, why not make a bit of cash while you're at it?)

Now that we have our piles of things we want to keep and a nice clean drawer to put them back into, place those items back in a way that makes sense to you. For the things you want to throw away, put them in the trash never to be seen again. For the things you want to donate, place those in a bag and drive it to the donation bin now (remember to include that time as part of the project when you're thinking about being Timebound, above). And for the things you want to sell, take some photos and post them on an online marketplace to sell, right away, don't wait. The aim is for those three piles to leave your home as soon as possible, for two reasons: to remove the temptation of changing your mind and because you don't want a bag of *more* clutter around the house when the goal is to declutter. Good-bye, old charger cords that no longer serve you and hello, clean, organized drawer of AAA batteries you can find when you need them.

Taking everything out of one small section allows you to be critical of all the items and ruthless about what you really need and what you really don't. If you don't do that, you'll just be shuffling things around in the space and not actually organizing anything. If you just push aside that pile of dress pants to the back of your closet instead of taking them out, you might not realize that one of them is a size 2 pleated black corduroy pant that you haven't worn since the '90s because a) they're ugly and b) you haven't been a size 2 since the '90s.

It's as simple as that.

But if it's that simple, why haven't you done it before? Well, simple doesn't mean easy. If it was easy, you would have already done it. So, let's talk about the process, the barriers, and—most important—the solutions.

Get Messy but Not Distracted

Yes, you heard it right. Organizing does involve getting a little messy first. Like I've said before, when you pick your space, whatever the space, no matter how big or how small, I want you to remove everything in that space and survey its contents. The taking everything out strategy works the same for an entire room as it does for a single drawer. So, pick your space, take everything out, get messy and assess what you're working with, but most important, stay on task, because this is where our old friend distraction can pop by for a visit.

If you're anything like me, it's hard not to entertain distraction. The simple act of cleaning out your closet can sometimes turn into a movie-montage fashion show where you're trying on old clothing and singing to the imaginary crowd attending your bedroom concert. We're all guilty of it.

We've all experienced the nostalgic feeling of rediscovering those forgotten photo albums or the worst culprit . . . old yearbooks. They instantly bring a smile to your face and trigger an old memory.

REFRAIN!!! DON'T DO IT! PUT THEM DOWN! It can happen fast—and not quicksand fast, but falling-through-a-trapdoor fast. Little old innocent Memory Lane can send you on a detour down Where the Fuck Did the Day Go? Boulevard in a hurry. Mindless flipping through the pages of forgotten high school memories will quickly hurl you into an investigation abyss. Once you are into that box, it's almost impossible to get out. Seeing Cheryl Farmer in that class photo will instantly get you wondering . . . whatever happened to Cheryl Farmer? Did she peak in high school? What she's doing now? At this point it's too late. You have already crossed into the danger zone. Next thing you know you're on Facebook, typing in her name, hoping it's still Farmer. Oh look! There she is. You find out she did marry Mark Murphy after all and it looks like they have two kids. The plot thickens . . . in 2014 she and Mark split up and she clearly invested in a quality, celebratory boob job. She loves selfies, wine, inspirational quotes, and activewear. Wait . . . what were we doing?

I've gotten distracted like this many times while organizing, and to be honest sometimes it's the fun part—but it's also the part that could set you up to fail. So, if you know that you are prone to this type of distraction, allow time for it. If you've allotted time to specifically organize the yearbook drawer, then by all means, flip through the pages and reminisce, but keep your eye on the prize. You've set aside an hour to clean out and organize this space, so perhaps just take five minutes to flip through the pages of that yearbook, but then it's book down and back to the task at hand. You can investigate Cheryl's life path another time.

Now, you might think I've just taken the only joy out of organizing if you can't spend hours reminiscing, but there are other ways to keep you entertained while still getting the job done. You might be thinking you'll just pop Netflix on "in the background," but once that TV goes on, you're watching it. It doesn't matter that I've seen *Pretty Woman* 144 times—watching Richard Gere snap that necklace box closed will always be more interesting than wondering how the sliding door for Barbie's camper ended up in my daughter's sock drawer when it took me two hours and a painful blood blister to assemble that thing in the middle of the night two Christmases ago. I work best when listening to music or a podcast, which is in the background enough that I can stay on task but enough of a diversion that I don't feel so painfully bored. You know yourself. Pick something to have in the background that will keep you energized and motivated but not so enthralled that you want to stop what you're doing. Think of this as a healthy distraction that will make the time fly by.

Be Ruthless

If you're going to get organized, you are going to have to get rid of things. No, I'm not trying to make you into a minimalist and have your house looking and feeling like a sterile and vacant space with no personality, but I am going to get you to think about what items you have in your home and encourage you to get rid of the ones that no longer serve you. For some spaces this may be a few items here and there, and for other spaces you'll be taking a trunk-load of bags to the donation bin. Have you ever felt like you have the weight of the world on your shoulders? Well, it's not the world, it's all of your stuff. If the idea of getting rid of things feels scary, that's okay, you're allowed to feel that way. But believe me, parting with things that no longer serve you can actually do the opposite: It can free you. Sounds simple right? But remember what I said, simple doesn't mean easy.

Parting with things can feel like parting with a piece of yourself. Maybe that old blanket or teddy bear from your childhood is something you can't part with. It's okay to hold onto items that are truly sentimental, but does the trophy you won for a three-legged race at the fireman's picnic in 1979 or the ticket stub from the Depeche Mode concert you went to in high school actually serve you in any way?

Have you ever filled a bag to drop off at a local donation bin and had a brief second, third, or even fourth thought of regret or uncertainty before you could let it go? You know you don't need the stuff, you haven't used it in years, and the space you removed it from looks so much better. But for some reason, you still have a moment of hesitation. You have a little conversation with yourself before you can let it go. Do I need it? Should I keep it just in case? Am I being wasteful or thoughtless? You are not alone.

If you are having a hard time letting go of an item, put it in plain sight for a while. Yes, I said in plain sight. Seeing it often will have you thinking about it more often. It will be easier to decide if it actually serves you. Hidden or tucked away will have you forgetting about it and allowing it to stay and take up space. Out of sight, out of mind. In your sight, on your mind.

Understanding that **your memories are stored within you and not in your stuff** may help a little. With that being said, a physical possession can trigger memories. Try taking a picture of an item before letting it go. If you have a collection of something, try hanging onto your favorites and letting go of the others. When you let go of things, you not only free up physical space, but you also free up visual busyness and space, which will in turn free up mental space.

If you're holding onto something simply because you fear you may need it in the future, think about how many times you have used it in the past year. The more unused and unloved possessions we hang onto, the more bound we feel to them and end up devoting more time and energy to maintaining and storing them.

I'm a vegetarian but I cook a turkey once a year, so I do need a roasting pan. I use it annually; it serves me and therefore there's a good reason to keep it. If I never used it, it would have no utility and there would be no good reason to keep it. The key is determining what items actually serve you. If they don't, let them go. Clutter begets more clutter. But try to be honest with yourself. Do you need that T-shirt you got for participating in the charity walk-a-thon five years ago? These are not hypothetical questions; these are questions to ask yourself and try to answer honestly.

I get wanting a lot of clothes, truly, but there are only seven days in a week. Listen, nobody has more clothes than I do. I have had a Lululemon shirt in my closet for five years that I've never worn but refuse to get rid of. I hate the sleeves and I keep meaning to get it altered. It was $120, so it feels wasteful. But I have to be honest with myself: If it's been five years, what are the chances this imagined alteration is ever going to happen?

Is hanging onto the dress you splurged on but never wore somehow earning you your money back? Do you really want to torture yourself by keeping that pair of jeans just in case you lose weight? Do you really need all of those painting clothes for the one day a year you paint? If the answer to any of those questions is no, get them outta there. **Stop creating a function for things in order to justify keeping them.** This is a convenient tactic for hanging onto shit you really don't need. Less is more, almost always.

QUESTIONS TO ASK ABOUT EVERY ITEM YOU PICK UP

- Do I love it?
- Do I use it?
- Does it enhance my life?
- Would I pass it on to a loved one?

- Do I have more of the same item?
- Would I buy it again today if it broke?
- Would my life be more difficult without it?
- Do I have somewhere adequate to store it?
- Is its utility worth my time to clean and maintain?

BIGGEST CLUTTER CULPRITS

- Gifts: Let go of things you are holding onto because they were a gift. Realize that the gift has already served its purpose. Release yourself from the feeling of obligation to someone else. Its purpose was to symbolize love or thoughtfulness from the person who gave it to you. You've said thank you, felt the love, and are now free to let it go.
- Books: There are not many good reasons to keep your university textbooks or that romance novel you read five years ago that was good but isn't even in your top ten. Books are meant to be read and shared, not collect dust, so if the book has served its purpose for you, it's time to pass it on to someone who can enjoy it, just as you did.
- Your kids' schoolwork and art: I know, I know. I *know*. The very idea of getting rid of your kids' art can feel like you are throwing away your actual child. But I am here to tell you: It is okay to say good-bye to the snowman he made from socks four years ago.

Have one box set aside per kid to keep the most treasured items and take a picture of the rest and save it on a flash drive. The memories are forever but the things don't have to be.

- Mugs: From every tourist attraction you've visited on a road trip and every "you are the world's greatest (Insert your personal world's greatest title . . .)," I can guarantee you that mugs are taking up at least twice as much space as they should. Just remember that most mugs were given to you by people who didn't really know you, that's why they gave you a mug.

- Memorabilia: Mickey ears from Disney World, participation ribbon from the science fair in the fourth grade, the giant foam finger from the football game back in '93. You and I both know you don't go into a box and look at them often. It's time for them to go.

- Towels and bedding: We often have too many linens, especially with kids. Come up with a number of how many sets you actually need and use, then donate the rest. If you have kids, take my word for it, you'll need a few spares for those middle-of-the-night pee or puke incidents. Animal shelters are a great option for towels, and human shelters are perfect for extra sheet sets.

- Makeup and perfume: First of all, this stuff expires. Second of all, if you didn't like the way that perfume or the hand cream your best friend gave you smelled yesterday, you won't like how it smells tomorrow. Why not just cut to the chase and throw it out?

- Medication and sunscreen: Again, these expire, and these expiration dates are a matter of health and safety. Medications and sunscreens will become less effective over time, and expired medication can be dangerous. These need at least a yearly purge.

- Take-out containers: Holding onto a take-out container because it feels wasteful to get rid of it doesn't unwaste that item. If you're never going to reuse it, it needs to go.

- Water bottles: You probably have one from every conference you've ever been to and every gym you got roped into joining. It's okay to say good-bye to the ones you never use and only keep the ones you actually do.
- Kitchen gadgets and utensils: You don't need six spatulas, four corkscrews, three lemon zesters, and two different nut crackers. Think about what you use and what you need and get rid of the rest.
- Reusable bags: You need a few in the house, some in your car, maybe one or two in your purse, and that is it.

Stuff is just stuff. I'm a social worker, and earlier in my career I worked with kids who had experienced difficult home lives. Many of them had no possessions of their own. While out on excursions, a lot of them took flyers, business cards, and pamphlets at every opportunity. The things they took were of no use to them, but they were *theirs*. Things can make you feel safe and secure, but as they accumulate you suddenly find yourself with too much. What started as safety and security flips to having the opposite effect: stress, anxiety, being overwhelmed.

Take Breaks to Stay Energetic and Productive

Short ones! Like this entry! Then back to work!

Invest in Some Organizational Tools

Boxes, bins, baskets, canisters, crates, totes, containers, dividers, labels, hooks, holders, racks, shelfs, cabinets. Yes, yes, yes, I know, Pinterest really has us thinking we need all these shiny things to live in an organized home, but do we really? No, probably not. TV and social media will have you believing that visual perfection is more important than functionality. Yes, it's true there are many things that will help with organization, but let's not get carried away. The goal is not per-fection, the goal is organized functionality. If you're confused about what functionality means, believe it or not, you're already doing it. You're not storing your everyday drinking glasses behind your grand-mother's crystal, because that would be silly and impractical. We're just going to expand on that without overdoing it. What I'm getting at is that I'm not going to tell you that you need to go out and buy a whole bunch of supplies to be organized. That would be counteractive after I've just told you to reduce clutter. We're going to work with what's best for your space in a way that makes sense to you.

You don't need to come up with a complicated solution; anything can be an organizer. A lot of people use cutlery organizers in the bathroom for toothbrushes and toothpaste, or in a drawer for pens, pencils, scissors, batteries, etc. In my house, we use a sock-and-underwear organizer to store Tupperware lids. Forget about what things are named and what they are supposedly designed to do—just look at it and think about its functionality. Drawer organizers, com-partments, and boxes can be helpful because they create separation and a limit. For example, my pen compartment fits ten pens, so I shouldn't have forty. I shouldn't even have fifteen. This also gives me a visual cue to see if things are depleting and need to be replaced. If you organize with function front of mind, things will automatically look better, too.

If you *are* in need of some organizational tools, that is totally fine, but again, they are not key. The key is figuring out what works for you and your space; whatever that is, that's the right answer. These are some that I love:

- Collapsible laundry baskets: They store flat, so they take up very little space when they are not in use.
- Over-the-door shoe storage: These are great for lots of things, not just shoes, because they're just pockets. You can use them for socks, underwear, and belts if you're limited on drawer space; or hats, mittens, scarves, cleaning supplies, craft supplies—whatever you want!

- A non-skid lazy Susan: I just bought one for my cabinets because I don't want to put oil and other spillable items directly on the shelves, because they could potentially damage the cabinet. A lazy Susan also helps you easily access and maximize your space.
- Shelf dividers: For separating, organizing, and maximizing space
- Adjustable drawer dividers
- Sliding baskets for cupboards: These are great for accessing items in deeper cupboards.
- Shower caddies: Like the back of the door shoe storage, you can hook them anywhere and the uses are endless. It's great for those accessories that don't have a home: belts, sunglasses, watches, ties, etc.
- Baskets, bins, and boxes: These are the classic organizing tools. Think about where you'll be storing them. Do you need them to be stackable? Would it serve you if it was clear plastic or opaque? Are you happy with them open or do they need a lid? My recommendation would be to go for durability. It wins every time. If it's easier, add a label to these so you know what's inside.
- Clear pantry containers: Visible and easy to see when you need to replenish items such as flour, rice, and pasta.

The Keep-Up:
Think Before You Buy

Imagine for a moment that you're done. Every inch of your house is decluttered and organized, and you can find things and live in your space with ease. Feels good, doesn't it? Or does it? Maybe it also brings with it that small little worry of *How am I going to keep it this way?!?* And that brings me to my little friend I like to call "keep-up." The key to keeping up your organization is thinking before you buy.

QUESTIONS TO ASK YOURSELF BEFORE YOU BUY:

- Do I really need it?
- Why do I want it?
- Where am I going to put it when it's not in use?
- How easy is it to clean and maintain?
- Do I already have one, and if so, do I really need another?
- Is this a replacement, and if so, am I getting rid of the old one?

You have to think about why you want what you want, and that's a complicated question for most of us because shopping isn't just about need. Shopping can be emotional, it can be therapeutic—but overshopping can also lead to clutter, which can lead to anxiety, which can lead to having a house you don't feel comfortable in. A common example of overshopping is "It was on sale" buying. This is when you buy too much of an item that you use, or don't use at all, just because it was on sale. Great that the spaghetti sauce was on sale and you want to pick up a few extras, but if you buy forty-seven of them, where the hell are you going to store it and will you ever be able to use it all before it expires?

Sometimes we feel like we need every new gadget and tool—new things are fun!—but there is a big difference between need and want. When the line gets blurred, we can end up with a bunch of stuff that we thought we needed but don't. What might help is breaking it down into how a need and a want differ, just some food for thought. (Is it chart time? Yes, it's chart time.)

NEED	WANT
Required to survive and function	Can improve quality of life
Essential	Nonessential
Doesn't change over time	Changes over time
Unfulfilled can result in adverse outcomes	Desired but if not fulfilled will not produce adverse outcomes
All individuals have the same basic needs	Differs from person to person

When you're considering buying or upgrading to a new gadget, again, mindfulness is key. For example, I have a Vitamix, but new blenders come out all the time. So, I think to myself, *Does this new blender do something so special that renders mine useless?* If the answer is no, then I don't buy a new one.

I bought a Roomba because on TV, that thing glides through a house like a figure skater at the Olympics. Mine? It gets stuck on everything. It can't get down the stairs. I bought it to make my life easier, and it doesn't, so I hate it. And because I hate it, I never use it, and it's just another appliance sitting in my garage in the Island of Misfit Toys.

Most people don't use gadgets that are complicated to clean. It's great that I can whip up a smoothie in thirty seconds but when I have to take apart five hundred pieces to wash and put back together, it doesn't really seem worth it. If this is you, accept that about yourself. There's nothing wrong with it. It just means that appliances that require a lot of maintenance are not for you.

My mission is to get you to enjoy the time you spend in your home doing the things you enjoy. Buying a new gadget might seem like it'll help you enjoy your space, but before you purchase, follow the thought process through to the end. You know yourself better than anyone. If you really want something, get it! But pause first and consider how it fits into your life and your goal of feeling comfortable, organized, and relaxed in your home.

When it comes to organizing, hopefully it feels a little lighter. I've taught you the how, the why, and the keep-up—all you have to do now is go and do it. So remember what I said: one step at a time; you're not going to move mountains overnight. Start small and stick with it, be ruthless, be kind to yourself, but be realistic. You've freed yourself from the clutter-fuck, now let's get things clean as fuck.

CLEANING

This Is Where You
Roll Up Your Sleeves

. . .

WHEN I WAS YOUNG, LIKE MOST KIDS, I HAD CHORES. *Unlike* most kids, I loved having chores. I would clip my Sony Walkman onto my belt, slide in my Whitney Houston cassette tape, and get to work. One Saturday morning I was told to clean the hardwood floors. The vacuuming went off without a hitch, then I moved on to mopping. Everything was going swimmingly. After I finished the floors, I moved on to the wooden stairs connecting our kitchen and family room, wiping each step by hand. I made sure I got in between every railing picket. But still, they were not sparkling enough for my discerning little eye. I decided to give them one last spruce with Pledge.

"That should really give them a good shine," I thought. So I sprayed and I buffed until those stairs shined like the top of the Chrysler Building. I could see my own reflection. It said, *Good job, kid; you're a cleaning star.*

Later that evening my father had prepared himself a large bowl of ice cream to eat while he watched TV. Ice cream in hand, he made his way to the family room. When my father's sock hit the first step, he didn't just slide, he flew. That bowl of ice cream cannoned straight up and hit the ceiling while he shot through the air, missing the rest of the stairs and landing on the family room floor in what could only be described as a snow angel position.

You live and you learn not to use Pledge on stairs, meaning, you learn by making mistakes. (Also: *Sorry, Dad.*) In other words: My cleaning skills have come from years of trial and error.

What *is* cleaning, anyway? Tidying? Straightening up? *Picking up?* Wiping down? The word alone feels ominous, imbued with a sense of endless duration, as in, *I'll be spending the next 12 hours cleaning and then I'll indulge in a luxurious 15-minute break and then it's back to cleaning . . . for the rest of eternity.*

I like to think of it this way: There are big cleans and little cleans. There are deep cleans and everyday tidies. Sometimes you need one but not the other. Sometimes you can go long periods of time without a deep clean as long as you're tidying daily. Make sense? Not yet? That's fine. Let me explain.

I tidy every day, meaning I don't go to bed with toys on the floor and dishes in the sink. The only thing I really want to do in the morning before going to work is unload the dishwasher. So I run it every night, before I go to bed, so I have a clean slate every day. Then I don't end up with a backlog of dishes weighing on my mind. To do this I set aside an hour every night to do everyday tidies and I call it my hour of power. It's a daily time-structured commitment. You may not have an hour each day but choose what time you can commit to, set a timer, and do it daily. (Half an hour of power also rhymes, just saying.)

Other small everyday tidies: folding the blankets, hanging up clothes, straightening the cushions, wiping down the countertop of the bathroom or kitchen, maybe a sweep (not a vacuum or a mop—just a good old-fashioned everyday sweep). I'm not getting down and cleaning the legs of the dining room chairs or pulling out the stove so I can sweep underneath it. But maybe I am going through that pile of mail on the counter and putting it where it needs to go so that it doesn't become Everest-sized. I'm wiping around the dog bowl, putting out the recycling, emptying the kitty litter. Basically, I'm doing the little annoying tasks that take practically no time at all if you do them continually but can become paralyzing if you ignore them for too long.

If you're not regularly tidying, you might be familiar with that "Oh shit!" feeling when you hear an unexpected knock at the door. When a friend pops by or my kid's playmate shows up and her mom lingers by the door, am I going to do everything I can to keep her on the porch because I'm too embarrassed to invite her in? There's no judgment here. It does not take much for a space to get messy. My kids, for example, like to remove their socks and wing them wherever—the more random the better. I don't know why preadult feet get hot so rapidly, but apparently they do. Whatever's going on with their feet, the socks are constantly everywhere, so I like to pick those up whenever I see them. (And eventually, when they're a little older, they will of course be responsible for picking up their own damn socks.) Cleaning the house around the kids can feel like brushing your teeth while eating an Oreo.

On Saturdays, I do a deep clean. What I *don't* want to spend my Saturday doing is sorting through mail and picking up socks, because I also have to scrub the bathroom and Pledge the tables (and oh yeah, work a full-time job, raise kids, and pay attention to my wife). If

throughout the week I'm preparing for the big clean with little cleans, the big clean gets less big. It's a time-saver because I'm spreading it out and taking off some of the mental weight. I want you to have a life outside of cleaning and work. I want you to look forward to the weekend. No one ever said, "TGIF so I can clean all weekend." No one. I can't give you an exact time on how long it'll take you to deep-clean your home as it depends on your keep-up routine. What I can tell you is what I keep telling you: The more time you spend keeping up, the less time you'll have to spend catching up.

What Kind of Cleaner Are You?

How you clean probably depends on your personality. You might fall into one of these categories:

- The Target Cleaner: You are someone who gets so over-whelmed by how many things there are to do that you decide to start with just one thing and you're all in. For example, the fridge. You take everything out, wipe it all down, and before you know it, you've alphabetized the condiments, perfectly lined up your bottles of water, all labels facing out, and polished the refrigerator doors. By the end of the day, the fridge is a chef's kiss, but the rest of the house is still a shit-stack. Sometimes target cleaning works great, and sometimes it becomes an avoidance tactic.

- The Panicker: You clean for a deadline and can work with remarkable gusto when the deadline is approaching. Your home might be a Monet, meaning that it looks great from afar but far from great up close. Your closets, cupboards, and drawers might be a disaster.
- The Surface Cleaner: Everything is clean enough. If you can't see underneath or behind it, it doesn't matter. This is the good-enough vibe.
- The Purger: You are someone who keeps everything until you're so frustrated that you snap. You are a slow accumulator . . . until the moment comes when you try to purge everything in one fell swoop. This is the "it's not clean unless it's empty" vibe.
- The Noncleaner Cleaner: You are the "what's the point of cleaning if it's just going to get messed up again?" cleaner. You mainly care about the dishes and laundry and anything else that is an absolute necessity for survival.
- The Distracted Cleaner: You start out with energy and the best of intentions. You're pulling out and sorting everything . . . until you're not. You are like a dog who just saw a squirrel, and there is no coming back for you. You fall deep into the distraction pit of photos and letters and mix tapes, oh my. Things are usually messier at the end than when you started, and you actually feel *more* overwhelmed.
- The Shuffler: You feel accomplished if a once-messy area is now clean, which is great. But: You only made one room tidy by moving the mess into another one (or a closet or under the bed). You spend lots of time and energy moving, shifting, and

shuffling things around without actually (sorry) accomplishing anything.

- The Martha Stewart: You pride yourself on spending a lot of time tidying and deep cleaning. You thrive on aesthetics. You love baskets and bins that match and functional is your middle name. Everything is lined up and color-coded; everything has a spot; all labels are facing out. You feel anxious if there is an empty spot in the coffee pod holder or the toilet paper display pyramid. You know where everything is and can find anything in a jiffy. You are a worker bee and fill downtime with new cleaning and organizing projects with little rest, but at the cost of what.

Here's the most important thing I want you to take away from this section and the entire book in general: My approach can help every type of cleaner, so knowing what type you are can help you navigate your inclinations. My guess is that you're probably looking to change *something*, or you wouldn't have bought this book. Take a moment to figure out what your goals are. Base your action plan on the level of cleanliness you are trying to achieve, which will help you reach your desired outcome. Just get started because that's the hardest part. No matter your cleaning style, no matter how much motivation you have, I guarantee that the biggest stumbling block for almost anyone is the getting started part; after that, you're off and running.

TOOLBOX

First, a disclaimer, one I will continue to make: Don't worry if you don't recognize some of the items on this list. Waste not one moment fretting if I have named some so-called crucial tool that you have never in your entire life heard of. Even if you have to google the word "soap," you are in the right place. Also, in some places I've listed brand names of products in case you're curious about what I specifically like. If you prefer generics or have other brand loyalties, follow your bliss!

Basic Tools Everyone Needs

- Vinegar
- Baking soda
- Toilet bowl cleaner (I like a swan-neck toilet cleaner)
- Dish soap (Dawn is my favorite)
- Scrubbing brushes (multiple sizes and stiffnesses)
- Lemon juice
- Microwave-safe bowl
- Mop and bucket (a spin mop is my favorite)
- Disinfectant wipes (Lysol's are my favorites)
- Plastic sandwich bags
- Rubber bands
- Vacuum
- Spray bottle
- Microfiber cloths (Maker's Clean are my favorites)
- An old sock
- Rubber gloves
- Window and glass cleaner (store-bought or DIY, I'll teach you how!)
- Cornstarch
- Glass cooktop cleaner (obviously only if you have a glass-top stove)

- Single-edge razor blade
- Squeegee
- Hydrogen peroxide
- Salt

IF YOU WEAR RUBBER GLOVES TO CLEAN, YOU HAVE TO CLEAN THOSE, TOO!

Think about it: If you were wearing rubber gloves to clean toilets, tubs, and other unsavory areas of your home, you definitely want to wash those before throwing them back under the sink. (On the other hand, maybe you're someone who throws out your rubber gloves after a few uses so you don't have to!) To clean them, wearing the gloves, just wash them as though you were washing your hands, with soap and water. Then dry them off. If you've been wearing them for a while, the insides have probably gotten sweaty and wet. Pulling them off usually leaves them partially inside out. To turn the glove completely inside out so you can wash and dry it, using both hands, pull the cuff outward on either side and spin the glove toward you a couple of times, then pop out the fingers like a balloon, then simply wash and dry. Repeat the process to turn them right side in and store them in a cool, dry place, out of direct sunlight.

Tools for More Advanced Cleaners Ready to Make Housework Their Bitch

- Shaving cream
- Tennis balls
- Bleach
- An old pillowcase
- Eye protection
- Face mask
- Drop cloth
- Pumice stone

- Rubbing alcohol
- Borax
- Melamine foam (Magic Eraser is my favorite)
- Can of compressed air
- Bar Keepers Friend
- Paintbrush, basting brush, or sponge
- Dawn Powerwash
- Oven cleaner
- Olive oil or vegetable oil
- WD-40
- Wax paper
- Grout cleaner (Zep is my favorite)

THIS IS HOW WE DO IT

Okay, here we go, it's happening. You've got the arsenal of cleaning tools and it's you vs. your home and you can do it! We'll take it step-by-step.

You Don't Need Lots of Products

Says she who just gave you a two-page list! You may have felt that was quite extensive but when you take a closer look, a lot of those items listed are probably things you already have. You'll find I didn't give you 1,001 different cleaning products to go out and purchase because I don't feel there are many miracle potions out there that make cleaning any easier. The truth is, I don't use a zillion different products when it comes to cleaning, and you don't have to either. A drop of Dawn in a bucket can clean an entire floor. A little bit of vinegar, baking soda, and water will clean almost everything else (and we'll talk specifics in a bit). My point is that the key to getting the house clean and in order does not lie in some magical product you haven't discovered yet. Sustainability, and saving money and space, are also nice little side effects of making your own cleaners. Remember: A fresh, floral scent is not the sign of a clean house, it's just the sign of added fragrance.

Less Is More When It Comes to Chemicals

People tend to think that the more you can smell a product, the better it must be working. Not so. For example, if you're cleaning with bleach and your home smells like a swimming pool, you're using too much! (And also, crack the windows immediately!) Bleach is meant to be diluted with water; under no circumstances should you be using straight bleach. A little bit of most chemicals goes a long way. And most important, be very cautious when mixing more than one chemical cleaning product together. Certain combinations can create a toxic concoction:

- Bleach and vinegar = chlorine gas
- Bleach and ammonia = chloramine
- Bleach and rubbing alcohol = chloroform
- Hydrogen peroxide and vinegar = peracetic acid

Aim for Progress, Not Perfection

We're all busy people with way too many responsibilities to possibly fit in one day, which is one of the main reasons cleaning can often get pushed to the back burner but stays on the front of your mind. Even if you're like me and enjoy cleaning, the process is never perfect—we all get interrupted or distracted or fed up with the repetitiveness. The key is to remember that doing *something* is better than doing nothing. If today all you do is wipe down your bathroom counter before bed when yesterday that would have seemed like a Herculean task, congrats: You're already succeeding.

Pencil It In . . . with a Big Black Sharpie

Without a plan that involves committing to regular scheduled time— like, *I'm going to clean for an hour every night before bed* or *Every morning before breakfast, I'll do a quick tidying*—you're liable to get swallowed up by the sheer idea of all that work and put it off entirely. A schedule will kick procrastination in the ass! The result of procrastination is what can cause us to feel overwhelmed and daunted by doing it all at once. Have you ever thought, I'm going to spend the whole day cleaning the house from top to bottom, and then I'm going to have a clean slate and get on top of cleaning from now on, only to get tired halfway through and give up until next time, only to *then* spiral into self-hatred and shame? Be realistic about how much time you have. If you have ten minutes, that's enough to do *something*—and something is really something. However, having a regular set schedule that you stick to is all part of the keeping-up plan. Setting aside one hour a day to clean and tidy might seem like a tall ask, but compared to eight hours on a Saturday it suddenly seems like the better option. Think of it in terms of a pie (I love pie): It makes more sense to have a slice a day for a whole week than to eat the whole pie on a Saturday in one sitting. Breaking down a large task into more manageable pieces will make an insurmountable task more achievable and less intimidating. So pencil it into your regular schedule, so you can have your pie and eat it, too, just not all at once.

Cleaning vs. Disinfecting

Cleaning is the process of removing dirt and germs from a surface. It does not necessarily kill germs, but by removing them, it lowers their numbers and the risk of spreading infection. Cleaning alone will only remove a very small number of germs and disturb their environment so it's harder for them to reproduce.

Disinfecting is the process of using chemicals to kill most (99.9 percent) of germs on hard, nonporous surfaces and objects. Disinfecting does not clean dirty surfaces. It kills germs and almost always requires a certain amount of prolonged sit time on a surface to do its job.

Keep in mind that you can clean without disinfecting, but you can't disinfect without cleaning.

The areas and items in your home that should be disinfected on a regular basis are referred to as high-touch points. Some of the most common high-touch points are:

- Doorknobs and cabinets
- Handrails
- Light switches
- Soap dispensers
- Taps
- Toilets
- Chair arms
- Tables and countertops
- Phones, television remotes, and electronics
- Toys
- Laundry hampers
- Refrigerators and dishwashers

HOW TO SANITIZE YOUR SPONGES

Two of the easiest ways to eliminate germs (99.9 percent) and clean sponges is by either running them in the dishwasher with your next load on the hottest/longest cycle or putting them in the microwave. Wet the sponge (without a plastic scouring pad) with water (not dripping) and microwave it on high for about 30 seconds to 1 minute. Let the sponge cool for another minute in the microwave before touching. I like to do this once a day, but minimally every few days. When your sponge is starting to degrade and fall apart, it's time to toss it.

Always Wipe in an S-Pattern

When it comes to wiping down any surface, use an S pattern. Avoid wiping in circles or back and forth so you're not rubbing dirty over clean. The same goes for mopping, which is in essence just wiping down a really big surface.

Paper Towels Are Not for Cleaning

Yes, they are convenient and great for wiping up spills, but paper towels leave lint behind, are expensive, and terrible for the environment. Instead, stock up on microfiber cloths and you'll cut down the amount of paper towels you need, saving you precious moolah, too. (When it comes to laundering your microfibers, never, ever use fabric softener: The buildup will stop their ability to absorb.)

Fabric Refresher Is Fine but It's Not a Cleaner

Fabric refresher is great as a refresher in between washes, but it doesn't remove soil. If I have fabric that smells super bad, I clean it. Fabric refresher is a chemically scented liquid; some refreshers will fight odors at the source while others will just sit on top of the fabric. These products do not remove the odor molecule but they do trap them and lessen their detection until they can be eliminated with a thorough cleaning. When it comes to fabrics—like curtains, carpets, furniture, and accent pillows—you are going to have to clean them once in a while.

A NOTE ABOUT BAKING SODA AND VINEGAR

Even the natural products we use for cleaning, like baking soda and vinegar, have chemical properties. Separately they have amazing cleaning power, but together, they will chemically react. Without getting too science-y, baking soda is a base and vinegar is an acid. They are on opposite ends of the pH scale. When used together, baking soda and vinegar will neutralize each other, basically canceling out the benefits of the low pH of vinegar and the high pH of baking soda. The chemical reaction will cause fizzing and bubbling that most of us are familiar with. (Remember the erupting volcano science project from your childhood?) The reaction between the vinegar and the baking soda produces bubbles of carbon dioxide gas that can be helpful in the cleaning process; however, it is **only** during that reaction time that it is in fact helpful. Once the cool fizzing and bubbling stop, you're basically left with salt water. This is why combining them in a bottle as a cleaner would be ineffective. The best and most effective way to use the two together is to use the baking soda first, allow it to sit and work its magic, *then* add the vinegar and quickly get to work.

Big-Clean Energy vs. Little-Clean Energy

As I mentioned earlier, **there are big cleans and there are little cleans. They are symbiotic: The more little cleans you do, the easier your big cleans will be.** Now I'm going to spell it out for you, give you practical examples so there's no confusion of what constitutes a little clean and a big clean. This is just a starter list, feel free to add to it things that apply to your home.

LITTLE CLEANS (Everyday Cleans)	BIG CLEANS (Deep Cleans)
Wiping down countertops in kitchens and bathrooms	Vacuuming/mopping
Putting away any loose items, e.g., mail, toys, stray socks	Full bathroom clean and disinfect
Folding throw blankets	Appliance cleaning—in, out, and underneath
Cleaning as you cook	Baseboards
Loading and unloading dishwasher (or washing your dishes if you don't have a dishwasher)	Getting rid of cobwebs and dusting indoor plants
Wiping down the stovetop	Cleaning windows and mirrors
Sweeping	Detailed dusting
Emptying garbage and recycling as needed	Kitchen—full clean and disinfect
Spot-cleaning food spills on cabinets or floors	Cleaning ceiling fans, light fixtures, and blinds
Pet maintenance—kitty litter, dog bowls	

Follow an Order of Operations
(Remember PEMDAS in Math Class?)

Work within a structured pattern or order. Organize your supplies and get ready. The best and most efficient method is cleaning top to bottom, left to right in every room. This is how professional cleaners clean. It's why they're able to clean an entire house in a few hours. It's an efficient and proven system and now it's about to become yours.

When you don't have an order of operations, cleaning is less efficient because you'll miss spots, and you'll spend a lot of time going back and forth, possibly going over the same surface twice. For example, in the kitchen, your first step would be giving yourself access to the surfaces you are about to clean by putting things away. Start at the left side of the room at the top. Clean the cabinets, shelves, appliances, lights, or fans; then move on to the counters; then work your-self down to the lower cabinets, dishwasher, etc.; and finish with the floors to scoop up whatever's fallen there during the cleaning process. I always finish with the floors. You want to clean yourself out of the room. This method is particularly good for distracted cleaners, be-cause it gives you a road map.

Have you ever noticed how fast professional cleaners work? It's because they don't double back, and that's efficient. You start at the top and knock the dirt down to the bottom; then you do the floor last. Logic should prevail while you work, and the most logical way is the one where you don't have to repeat yourself. It's where the expression "from top to bottom" comes from.

Spread Things Out over Time

The same rule of thumb that applies to organizing applies to cleaning: Set reasonable goals and start small. For example: Can you clean the entire inside of your fridge today? If you said yes, great. If your most realistic answer is no, how about just the produce and fruit drawers? If not, what about just the salad-dressing shelf? Remember: It takes a long time to accumulate dirt and grime, so why wouldn't it take a long time to get rid of it? Be kind to yourself.

Divide and Conquer

Remember my nan? She cooked, cleaned, polished, and painted. But my grandfather had jobs, too. He did yard work and maintained the car. He would fix things here and there, but mostly he tinkered in the yard and in the garage. He was always there to grease my bicycle chain and pump my tires. He always made sure I had a new stiff piece of cardboard clothes-pinned to the fork of my bike so that it sounded like a motorcycle as I peddled and it hit against the spokes. He always had the perfect piece of plywood and a brick to make a jump for me to launch my bike off (little Melissa, the BMX bandit).

Their system was to divide and conquer. Some people might pre-fer cleaning the kitchen since they cook more often, while others' strengths may be in the yard. Just like sports teams control the game by playing to people's strengths, members of a household can do the same thing. Think of the people in your household, whatever that looks like for you, as a team. Dividing the tasks among the team members doesn't necessarily mean that everyone will have the same number of tasks. Equality doesn't always mean equal. It's hard to place value on a task, but things to consider are time, effort, strengths, and interest.

How to Clean Specific Things

We are not going to get into machines here. Your dishwasher, your washer-dryer . . . they need a particular kind of cleaning that's more like maintenance (i.e., it keeps them functioning the way they are supposed to) and they will get their own section in the book (fancy). Here, we'll focus on how to clean the stuff in your house that gets the dirtiest and dustiest. It's loosely organized by room (starting with the bathroom), but certain things (floors, baseboards) exist in multiple rooms.

Toilets

I have to deep-clean my kids' bathroom every three days because you'd be surprised by what ends up where. There is a saying that "pee-

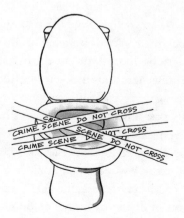

ing on the seat is like hitting the post on an empty net." I swear it's like they are actually aiming for the post. I have tried explaining to them that peeing is like being on a road trip ... the "aim" is to get from point A to point B, you need to follow the map, stay on the road, remember that it's much shorter than you think, and remain seated for the duration of the trip. Sometimes I think maybe I should have spent more time talking to rocks before I had kids—it would have been good practice as they have similar listening habits.

Before we even get into cleaning the toilet, let's talk about prevention. Close the lid! Training the kids, big and small, to close the lid before flushing will eliminate the fine spray of particles from the force of the flush into the air. Those particles would otherwise sit back, relax, and settle on walls, cabinets, counters, and floors, all while enjoying the easy listening waves of your gags while you clean them up.

Many of us wipe down the seat, use a cleaner in the bowl, then call it a day. That's a great start, but the base can be just as nasty and is one of the most commonly missed areas in the bathroom. Clean every part of your toilet thoroughly. It's one of the grossest things in your house.

Though it's first on the list, the toilet should be the last thing you clean in your bathroom, because you don't want to risk contaminating other parts of the bathroom with toilet germs. Your bathroom is a high-touch area. You want to make sure that the entirety is wiped down and disinfected, or you'll be spreading toilet germs to whatever you touch. (Again, gross.) Always read directions on store-bought cleaners and follow recommendations for "sit time." This is the amount of time the cleaner needs to sit on the surface to let the disinfectant do its job.

Consider turning off the water before cleaning the bowl. That way, when you flush after turning off the water, it stops it from refilling. Reducing the water level means that your cleaner won't be as diluted and will actually stick to the sides of the bowl, like it's supposed to. Once you're done scrubbing, turn the water back on and give the toilet one more flush.

HOW TO TURN OFF THE WATER SUPPLY

Turning off the water supply to the toilet is easier than it sounds: If you look down to the left or right of the base of your toilet, there should be a knob or a lever on the wall or the floor. Turn that knob as far to the right as you can until you stop hearing the flow of water and you're good to go.

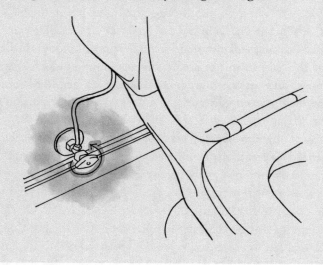

Wipes are fine for disinfecting everything but the bowl, just don't flush them. For the bowl, use a toilet cleaner, but if you have hard water, you may also need a pumice. (Think of it as the pumice stone the pedicurist uses on your callouses, except it's made specifically for cleaning toilets and other porcelain fixtures. It's abrasive enough to work, but gentle enough not to scratch.)

If you prefer something gentler than store-bought chemicals (i.e., the potentially harmful ingredients and irritating scent of bleach are just not how you roll), you can make your own solution:

1. Combine ½ cup water, ½ cup dish soap, ½ cup baking soda, and ¼ cup hydrogen peroxide (see Note) in a squeeze bottle. Give the solution a good shake.

2. Apply the entire solution to the toilet bowl as you would with the store-bought cleaner.
3. Allow it to sit for 10–15 minutes.
4. Scrub with a brush.
5. Flush and you're done!

Note: Hydrogen peroxide needs to be used right away once it's out of its brown bottle as it is light sensitive.

Mirrors

Spray glass cleaner (maybe your own homemade window cleaner, see below) and wipe the mirror down with a microfiber cloth. For bathroom mirrors, about once a month, add a second step to prevent fog: Apply a small amount of shaving cream to a microfiber cloth, apply it to the entire mirror, then buff it off with another clean microfiber cloth. (Wax on, wax off.) Take a look at your mirrors the next time you take a hot shower. Zero fog!

MAKE YOUR OWN CLEANER FOR WINDOWS, GLASS, AND METAL

There's no shame in buying your products at the store. If you're trying to save money and/or control the ingredients/chemicals in your home, homemade window cleaner is the easiest thing to try DIY (and it's not just for windows). All you need is:

- 2 cups water
- ¼ cup rubbing alcohol
- ¼ cup distilled white vinegar
- 1 tablespoon cornstarch—the secret ingredient that micro-scrubs without scratching

Put it in a spray bottle and mix it up. Label the bottle (see page 40). Boom, done.

Always label all bottles of homemade cleaning products or solutions that you plan to store and use later. If you notice a change in color, consistency, or odor (and this goes for store-bought stuff, too), it's time to replace it.

Also! With any cleaning product (homemade or store bought) it's imperative to always do a spot test. I know you have heard and read this a million times, but it's a must! Always test each product or solution on a small, inconspicuous spot on every surface or object you plan on cleaning before going all in.

Drains

A clogged or slow drain stinks (sometimes literally). When this happens, check for and remove hair and other grossness. Take out or pop up the drain cover, then sprinkle some baking soda into the drain and pour a little vinegar over the top. Give it a few minutes to do its sizzle magic, then let the hot water run to rinse it down.

Magic Erasers are truly magical (go figure). I can't live without them. I use them on almost everything because they take off dust, dirt, scuffs, and so on. It can look like you've repainted your doors or baseboards if you Magic Eraser them once in a while. I recently used them to remove tea stains from my countertop after helping my daughter with a history project that involved making papers look old by staining them with tea. Magic Erasers work because they're microabrasive, which means they do microscopic scrubbing, like very fine sandpaper. The magic is in the melamine. Melamine is both porous and dense. Where cleaners break down stains, melamine scrubs the stains off with very little elbow grease needed. When wet, the microscopic scrubbers become hard, and as they lift the dirt, it is pulled into the open spaces in the eraser. Think of it as a surface dirt exfoliator.

The foam is water activated, so you want to dampen it with water before getting to work. The Magic Eraser will degrade or wear away as you use it. It's far superior to a traditional sponge, so save them for more challenging stains and stick to soap and water for everyday spills. The Magic Eraser is not intended for delicate or glossy surfaces—remember, it is like very fine sandpaper.

Bathtubs

Step one is figuring out what type of tub you have. Most are acrylic, fiberglass, porcelain, or cast-iron (or sometimes steel). Firmly press your hand against the side of the bathtub: If it has a little give, it is likely made of acrylic or fiberglass. If it doesn't, it's likely porcelain or cast-iron. If it's one of the latter, grab a magnet and hold it against the wall of the tub. If it sticks, your tub is made of steel or cast-iron. If you have jets in your tub, ooh la la! (But also, I'll tell you how to clean those.)

One thing that applies to every kind of tub: Never use abrasive powders that contain bleach (like Ajax and Comet), or hard or stiff brushes. You'll risk damaging the tub.

Acrylic, fiberglass, and porcelain tubs

1. Mix 3 cups of water and ¼ cup Dawn dish soap in a spray bottle.
2. Spray an adequate amount of the Dawn and water solution on the tub surface.
3. Sprinkle a little baking soda around the tub.
4. Leave for 15 minutes.
5. Use a Magic Eraser or sponge to scrub.

6. Rinse with water.
7. Dry with a soft microfiber cloth.

Cast-iron tubs

1. Mix 2 cups water, ½ cup baking soda, and ¼ cup Dawn dish soap into a paste.
2. Spread the mixture on the tub surface.
3. Leave for 15 minutes.
4. Scrub with nonabrasive cloth or sponge.
5. Rinse with water.
6. Dry with a soft microfiber cloth.
7. If you have extra grime or a ring you can use a Magic Eraser without damaging the bathtub and rinse with water.

Jetted

Cleaning a jetted tub is an actual pain in the ass! Yes, it is. That's because you have to clean the tub *and* the jets, and the way you do each is different. (It's a catch-22: A jetted tub can bring relaxation, but all that relaxation may evaporate once you realize how often you have to clean it.) Most modern jetted bathtubs are equipped with a water purification system that pumps ozone (or energetic oxygen) into the water, which acts as a sterilizer to eliminate algae, mildew, mold, and bacteria in the water. But that's not enough to prevent mold, mildew, and bacteria from accumulating in the jets. You still have to clean the thing—jets and basin—pretty regularly.

Clean your tub jets at least every 3 months or more often depending on frequency of use. You can purchase a commercial cleaning solution suitable for jetted tubs or you can use bleach or distilled white vinegar.

Here's the cleaning process for the jets:

1. Fill the tub with water above the highest jet.
2. Pour in the commercial cleaning solution. (If you are not using a commercial solution, just add either ½ cup bleach

or ½ cup distilled white vinegar and 2 tablespoons low-sudsing dish soap.)

3. Let the jets run for 15 minutes.
4. Drain the tub and refill with clean water and run it again for 10 minutes.
5. Repeat the process if the water was extremely dirty or chunks of black grossness were floating in the water.
6. Drain and wipe down with water and a soft microfiber cloth.

Then, when it comes to cleaning the tub itself, just follow the instructions for acrylic and fiberglass tubs.

Showers

I know you don't want to hear this, and I genuinely hate to say it, but the truth is the best time to clean your shower is right after you use it. I know, I know! I can feel your eyes rolling. You just took a shower—you don't want to clean it! You're in a rush! And you feel all fresh and rejuvenated from the nice warm water. But here's the thing: The shower is already wet, and the steam has loosened up the grime for you, making your job much easier. If you can bear it, just do it right away before you have time to talk yourself out of it.

Fiberglass showers

1. Mix 3 cups of water and ¼ cup Dawn dish soap in a spray bottle.
2. Spray an adequate amount of the Dawn and water solution on the walls and base of the shower.
3. Sprinkle or toss a little baking soda onto the walls.
4. Leave for 15 minutes.
5. Rinse with water.
6. Dry with a soft microfiber cloth.
7. If you have extra grime or a ring, use a Magic Eraser and rinse with water.

Tile showers

1. Mix 2 cups of distilled white vinegar and ¼ cup Dawn dish soap in a spray bottle.
2. Spray an adequate amount of the solution to the tiles.
3. Leave for 15 minutes.
4. Scrub with a soft-bristled brush, mop, or sponge.
5. Rinse with water and dry with squeegee, microfiber, or towel. (To be honest I'm so proud that you made it this far, I don't care if you dry it with the sleeve of your hoodie.)

Stone showers

Stone showers like granite, marble, travertine, and other natural materials, need different cleaning attention because they are vulnerable to scratches and stains. Do not use harsh tile cleaners or acidic ingredients like vinegar or lemon juice, as these can damage the stone's surface.

1. Mix 3 cups of water and ¼ cup Dawn dish soap in a spray bottle.
2. Spray an adequate amount of the Dawn and water solution on the stone.
3. Sprinkle or toss a little baking soda onto the shower walls.
4. Leave for 15 minutes.
5. Rinse with water.
6. Dry with a soft towel or microfiber cloth.

Glass showers

To make it easy on yourself, make sure you squeegee the glass immediately after every shower to reduce water marks, streaking, and spotting. To make it even easier, make a DIY daily spray by mixing ½ cup of rubbing alcohol, 1 teaspoon of Dawn, 2 tablespoons of rinse aid, and about 3 cups of water into a spray bottle. Applying this spray followed by a squeegee after every shower will reduce the amount of big cleans you will need on the glass. For big cleans, use the following:

1. Spray your homemade glass cleaner or use Bar Keepers Friend cream cleanser on the glass.
2. Rinse it off and squeegee for best results.

Exhaust Fan

Depending on how old your home is and local building codes, you may have an exhaust fan. Go into the bathroom and look up. See that slatted rectangle in the ceiling? That's probably an exhaust fan. They are an important part of the home's ventilation system. They suck up moisture, humidity that can lead to mold and mildew growth, and eliminate odor. They exist almost exclusively in bathrooms, which get steamy, but if you live in an apartment building, you might also have one in your kitchen. To clean any of these, as soon as you start to see dust, turn off the fan, take off the slatted cover, and just rinse it under the tap until the water runs clear. That's how you'll know that it's ready to pull air through it again, which is what it's designed to do. You can also put it in the dishwasher for a quick clean. If there is dust buildup in the fan, you can dust or vacuum to ensure the fan can operate freely and easily.

Toilet Paper Holder

I'm guessing you've never thought about cleaning the toilet paper holder before, right? But you should actually disinfect it. Know why? Think about how many people touch it and what they're doing just before touching it. Eww. So yeah, wipes or any kind of disinfectant cleaner should get *all* up in that TP dispenser often.

Stainless Steel

All you need to clean and polish stainless is WD-40. Just spray it on a rag and wipe it in the direction of the grain. If you can't stand the smell of WD-40 (it'll go away, I promise), an alternative is to use vinegar and water or soap and water to clean the stainless, then use a bit of olive oil on a rag to polish.

WD-40 IS A UNICORN PRODUCT THAT YOU CAN USE FOR PRETTY MUCH EVERYTHING

It was invented in 1953 by the Rocket Chemical Company, and it stands for Water Displacement Formula 40. These are just a few of the things it can do:

- Clean and polish stainless steel
- Lubricate shovels, hoes, and garden trowels so snow and dirt slide right off
- Clean up makeup, nail polish, paint, and scuff marks from tile
- Remove gum from hair
- Soften and protect leather
- Remove rust and prevent it from re-forming
- Remove sticker residue
- Stop wooden tool handles from splintering
- Unstick and loosen stuck zippers
- Remove crayon
- Polish gold, brass, and chrome
- Remove candle wax, ink, and glue from your carpet
- Loosen rusty nuts and screws
- Remove tree sap and bird poop from your car
- Keep insects off windows and stop them from building nests
- Unstick your fingers if you accidentally superglue them together
- Help get off rings stuck on your fingers
- Remove tea stains from countertops
- Repel bugs
- Remove lime scale and grime from toilets
- Degrease your hands (just wash with soap and water after)
- Remove yellow haze from your headlights
- Clean and renew color on plastic patio furniture
- Kill prickly weeds like bull thistle and Russian thistle

Glass Shower Doors and Metal Accessories (like Shower Heads and Faucets)

That homemade window cleaner (see page 39) can also be used for polishing taps, glass, and metal with a microfiber cloth. A piece of wax paper can also, surprisingly, be used to polish the above with some vigorous rubbing.

Baseboards and Blinds

For the baseboards in the bathroom—where humidity from the shower or tub creates a sort of adhesive effect—dampen a cloth and wipe over the surface. In other rooms where humidity isn't a factor, you can simply just dry dust. If they get dirt and scuffs, the Magic Eraser is the perfect weapon. It makes them look new, like a paint job, especially if your baseboards are white.

Slatted blinds get dusty and are a pain to clean. There is no need for a fancy tool to clean them, your hand is the perfect solution. The easiest way is just to grab a sock, slightly dampen it, put it over your hand, grasp each slat, and glide it along from one side to the other. If your blinds need a super deep clean, you can give them a bath. Yes, that's right. If the slats and cords are heavily soiled and discolored, you can give them a good soak in the tub with dish soap and water.

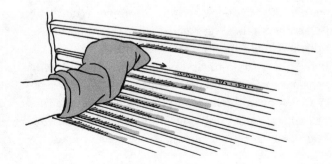

TVs

Avoid glass cleaners or other household cleaning products because they contain ammonia or alcohol and over time those can damage the antireflective, antiglare coating on the screen. Also stay away from paper towels and napkins, which are abrasive and can scratch the screen and leave lint behind.

1. Turn off and/or unplug the TV.
2. You can buy screen wipes or cleaners, but all you really need is a clean microfiber to do a dry dust. You could even use an eyeglass cleaning cloth—I know you have a bunch and, let's be honest, you don't actually use them on your glasses.
3. Use a can of compressed air to clean the casing and around the back.
4. Spray some distilled water onto your cloth and apply very light pressure as you wipe in a circular motion. (Add a drop of dish soap—1 part soap to 100 parts water—if there are greasy fingerprints on the screen.)
5. Buff it off with a dry cloth.

Refrigerator

Start by taking everything out. If you've got soy sauce and ketchup pooled and encrusted in the door shelf, it will be very hard to remove it if you don't take everything out. This goes for all the shelves and drawers, most of which are removable, so take out what you can and wash them with soap and water for a thorough clean. Trying to dab into weird corners at awkward angles while the fridge beeps at you for being open too long is no way to live.

You don't have to do this every time you open the fridge or even any time you want to spruce up the fridge a little (meaning sometimes it's okay to just open the door and run a wipe over the surfaces), but consider that soy sauce pool a sign from above: When you see it, it's time to take everything out. You can use whatever you want to clean—soap and water or a wipe.

Trash Cans and Recycling Bins

Mix a few drops of dish soap and water in the bin, then use a toilet brush or other long brush to scrub off the nasty from the sides and lid. Repeat the process until clean. Rinse, wipe dry, and you're done.

STUFF YOU PROBABLY DIDN'T KNOW YOU CAN CLEAN IN THE DISHWASHER

First things first: "Dishwasher-safe" isn't an industry standard definition. It's just a general consensus of what can withstand high heat, detergent, and water pressure. So, here is a nonexhaustive list of things you might not have known you can toss in your dishwasher:

- Toothbrush holders
- Shower poufs
- Sponges (including Scrub Daddys)
- Exhaust fan covers
- Dog collars
- Leashes
- Microwave turntables
- Light-fixture covers
- Hairbrushes and combs (remove hair first)
- Manicure and pedicure tools
- Plastic or rubber bath toys or pet toys
- Silicone oven mitts
- HVAC vent grates
- Golf balls
- Flowerpots
- Unlined rubber boots
- Flip-flops
- Keys (no fobs)

The best part is that you don't have to do a special keys-and-flip-flops load. You can mix and match that stuff with your regular dishes, because it's all getting cleaned. If this grosses you out, then separate them, but cleanliness-wise, there's no reason to.

What are some things that should never, ever go in the dishwasher? Wood, cast-iron, nonstick pans, and copper.

Counters

Different types of counters require different methods of cleaning, disinfecting, and spot-cleaning.

Granite counters

- To clean, use warm water and dish soap on a nonabrasive sponge.
- To disinfect, add a half-and-half mixture of rubbing alcohol and water to a spray bottle. Spray down the entire surface and let it sit for at least 5 minutes. Dry it with a clean cloth and it's disinfected.
- To spot-clean, sprinkle a small amount of baking soda on the stain, rub it in with a wet nonabrasive sponge, and then wipe it off.

Butcher block counters

- To clean, use warm water and dish soap on a nonabrasive sponge, going in the direction of the grain.
- To disinfect, put distilled white vinegar on a microfiber cloth, wipe it on the surface, leave it for 10 minutes, then wipe it off.
- To spot-clean, make a paste with salt and lemon juice, apply it to the stain, rub it in with a wet nonabrasive sponge, and then wipe it off.

Concrete counters

- To clean, use warm water and dish soap on a nonabrasive sponge.
- To disinfect, add a half-and-half mixture of rubbing alcohol and water to a spray bottle. Spray down the entire surface and let it sit for at least 5 minutes. Dry it with a clean cloth and it's disinfected.
- To spot-clean, sprinkle a small amount of baking soda on the stain, rub it in with a wet nonabrasive sponge, and then wipe it off.

Laminate counters

- To clean, use warm water and dish soap on a nonabrasive sponge.
- To disinfect, combine 2 cups water with 2 tablespoons vinegar in a spray bottle. Spray down the entire surface and let it sit for at least 3 minutes. Dry it with a clean cloth and it's disinfected.
- To spot-clean, sprinkle a small amount of baking soda on the stain, rub it in with a wet nonabrasive sponge, and then wipe it off.

Quartz counters

- To clean, use warm water and dish soap on a nonabrasive sponge.
- To disinfect, add a half-and-half mixture of rubbing alcohol and water to a spray bottle. Spray down the entire surface and let it sit for at least 5 minutes. Dry it with a clean cloth and it's disinfected.
- To spot-clean, sprinkle a small amount of baking soda on the stain, rub it in with a wet nonabrasive sponge, and then wipe it off.

Marble counters

- To clean, use warm water and dish soap on a nonabrasive sponge. Important to note, no lemon juice, no vinegar. Marble is vulnerable to acidic liquids and cleaners.
- To disinfect, add a half-and-half mixture of rubbing alcohol and water to a spray bottle. Spray down the entire surface and let it sit for at least 5 minutes. Dry it with a clean cloth and it's disinfected.
- To spot-clean, sprinkle a small amount of baking soda on the stain, rub it in with a wet nonabrasive sponge, and then wipe it off.

Stainless steel counters

- To clean, use warm water and dish soap on a nonabrasive sponge.

- To disinfect, combine a half-and-half mixture of distilled white vinegar and water in a spray bottle. Spray down the entire surface and let it sit for at least 5 minutes. Dry it with a clean cloth and it's disinfected.
- To spot-clean, sprinkle a small amount of baking soda on the stain, rub it in with a wet nonabrasive sponge, and then wipe it off.

Microwaves

Don't neglect it! The longer you ignore a nasty food splatter, the stinkier it will be and the harder it will be to clean. Microwaves are deceptively difficult to clean because you need to pretzel your body into strange positions to get in there, but go ahead, get in that box. I can't give you an exact cleaning schedule because it depends on your

particular household habits. If your kids are like mine, they love to cook ravioli with no cover so that the sauce splatters everywhere. So, I wipe down my microwave almost every time they use it. If I don't wipe it down straightaway my next meal of potato soup will also have a hint of yesterday's ravioli flavor. Once my children are all out of the house, I expect to spend a lot less time cleaning up their microwave masterpieces.

The easiest way to clean and refresh your microwave requires very little elbow grease.

1. Add 1 cup of distilled white vinegar and 2 tablespoons lemon juice (optional) to a microwave-safe bowl or mug.
2. Place the bowl or mug in the microwave and run it for 2 to 3 minutes.

3. Let the bowl sit for 30 seconds before removing, then wipe the interior with a wet cloth.

DON'T OPEN THE MICROWAVE DOOR BEFORE THE BEEP

Are you that person? Do you dive across the kitchen with little to no regard for anything or anyone in your path in order to stop the microwave before the well-known, well-despised beep? Does it give you that satisfied but out of breath relief of "I made it" feeling? Do you feel like James Bond in *Goldfinger* stopping the clock on the atomic bomb before it hits 0:00, saving the world as we know it from complete destruction? Well let's talk about your mission.

The safety shutoff in your microwave is there to prevent accidents. The real risk is to the microwave. If you open the door while the microwave is running, you are interrupting the power circuit. It's not good for the motor or the door switches. If the microwave is still running when you pull the door open, the microswitches in the door latch system suddenly cut power to the transformer. When this occurs, there is a spark across the switch. Over time this may reduce the life of the switch and the microwave. As for your personal safety, it is completely safe to open the door while the microwave is running.

Stoves

An ounce of prevention works wonders! If you wipe up spills and food as you go, you'll be saving yourself a world of pain. If you leave spills and food (that random piece of pasta that escaped the pot or that tomato sauce that simmered on high for too long) on your stovetop and then use it again, you're recooking the food, which is going to make it harder to remove eventually. So, make sure to clean after every use to avoid the seemingly unbreakable crust.

Take apart as much as you can. In the same way that it's more effective to take everything out of the fridge to clean it instead of wiping around the milk carton and broccoli stalks, for ovens, stoves, and grills, you should remove as many parts as you can: racks, burner covers, etc. Just be careful with a gas stove: If you get the burners wet, they won't light until they dry out.

Gas range

Cleaning gas ranges is not fun. I've got one and although it looks great, I hate it just a little because of the time it takes to clean it. The toughest parts to clean are the grates. First, remove those grates and the burner covers. If they have a lot of built-up food and grease, you can use an oven cleaner, just remember to be in a well-ventilated area when doing it. A more natural way of cleaning the grates is allowing them to soak in warm water and use a wet pumice. After doing that, set those aside to dry and clean the top itself. Use Dawn Powerwash or sprinkle baking soda and spritz with water on hard to remove spots, rinse it off, and give it a once-over with a cloth. Now that you've buffed, it's time to shine: For your grates and burner covers, once they're dry, rub in a little olive oil or vegetable oil.

Glass-top range

For a glass-top range, be sure to treat the glass cooktop with TLC. Forget the pumice scouring stone here. Instead, opt for a stovetop cream cleaner, which is microabrasive, so it's effective but won't scratch. For a more natural clean, sprinkle with baking soda and then spritz it with some water and let sit, then simply wipe off. For difficult to remove baked-on food and grease, use a single-edge razor blade or a Magic Eraser. (If you prefer to use distilled white vinegar instead of water, remember, when using baking soda and vinegar together, it is only during the reaction time that it is helping to loosen the grime.)

Electric burners

If you have an electric range, remove the burners and set them aside. Clean the tops with Dawn and water, or Dawn Powerwash. For a more natural clean, sprinkle with baking soda and then spritz it with some water and let it sit, then simply wipe off. Then put the burners back in.

For all of these ranges, you can also use window cleaner (or your homemade window cleaner; see page 39), on the front of the appliance and the viewing window. But beware: If you have a stainless appliance with painted-on numbers, commercial window cleaner may remove them! So don't just spray it willy-nilly; use it strategically and carefully or, if you want to play it safe, just use a damp microfiber cloth.

Ovens

Self-cleaning ovens

Use the self-cleaning option if your oven has one. That's what it's for! FYI, the cycle could take up to 4 hours and it will lock you out unless you cancel the cycle and won't open until it returns to a safe temperature. Also, your racks can yellow in the self-clean phase, so take them out (we'll get to how to clean those in a sec). How often you self-clean your oven depends on how dirty it is. If you can wipe stuff out, do that. Staying on top of it can reduce the need to do a self-clean as often, which can save you a little on the power it takes for that process. I prefer to be home and awake while I am running a self-cleaning cycle. You don't want a fire in your oven because you dropped a few French fries. You should use commercial oven cleaner sparingly on a self-cleaning oven. Continuous use of chemical cleaners on a self-cleaning oven liner may cause etching and discoloration of the liner. Eventually, this will cause the oven to not clean effectively when using the self-clean cycle. It's the heat that cleans, it turns everything to ash. You will still have to clean your window, but the inside should be a chef's kiss.

Lastly and most randomly, the fumes from self-cleaning ovens can be lethal to birds. It is recommended that you move your pet birds to another part of the house to keep them safe. Having them outside during the process is the safest. A better option is to refrain from using the function and to clean the oven with baking soda, water, and a little bit of elbow grease. This will keep your pets and family even safer!

Oven racks

When self-cleaning an oven, the temperature will become significantly higher than the typical temperatures used for cooking. Leaving the racks in the oven during the self-cleaning process can cause discoloration, dull the finish, and damage the coating that allows the racks to slide in and out with ease.

I know you are not going to want to hear this, so brace yourself: It is best to remove the racks and clean them the old-fashioned way with a bit of elbow grease and determination. For any type of oven, here are two of my favorite and most effective methods of cleaning oven racks:

COMMERCIAL OVEN CLEANER: **Most commercial oven cleaners produce toxic fumes, so it's always best to clean your racks outside if possible. There are many options, including fume-free.**

1. Before you begin you will want rubber gloves, eye protection, and a mask.
2. Start by covering a work surface with a drop cloth, towels, or trash bags and place the oven racks on top.
3. Spray the oven cleaner liberally onto the racks ensuring that they are completely covered. Let sit for 15 to 20 minutes. Flip the racks over and repeat.
4. Scrub the racks with a cloth, Magic Eraser, or a medium stiff brush. Rinse thoroughly and dry.

BAR KEEPERS FRIEND: **This method is a great alternative to using oven cleaner if you are at all concerned with toxicity.**

1. Start by making a paste using powder Bar Keepers Friend and water. The paste should be thick enough to apply with a brush. Alternatively, you can use Bar Keepers Soft Cleanser, eliminating the need to make a paste.
2. Place the racks in a sink or tub. (This can be done outside if you prefer.)

3. Use an old paintbrush, basting brush, or sponge to apply the Bar Keepers on the front and back sides of the racks. Let sit for 45 minutes.
4. Scrub the racks with a cloth, Magic Eraser, or a medium-stiff brush. Rinse thoroughly and dry.

Ceiling Fans

Grab an old pillowcase, put each individual blade inside the pillowcase one at a time (you'll likely need to bunch up the loose material at the opening), then pull it back and off the blade. This way, you capture all the dust within the pillowcase instead of having it fall to the floor or float all over the room and your face.

Hardwood, Laminate, and Vinyl Floors

Two reasons people started to steer away from carpet and toward hard flooring, especially hardwood, are that 1) hard flooring is easier to keep clean and 2) it reduces the potential allergens in your home. Varnish and polyurethane (as opposed to just straight wood stain) act as a protective barrier against water and dirt in real wood flooring, so that's another pro. Carpets need to be vacuumed regularly and steam-cleaned semiregularly, because they're a magnet for common allergens like dust, pet dander, and pollen. Wall-to-wall carpeting traps odors (like pet urine or spilled milk or wine) underneath and into the underpad.

Some hardwood manufacturers recommend using a mop dampened with water only. As always, read and follow the manufacturer's instructions so you don't risk voiding the warranty.

When it comes to hard flooring:

- Think less is more, especially when it comes to wood. This is particularly important when it comes to water. A soaked or wet mop can ruin the finish and damage the wood. Same goes for laminate, which is essentially just compressed wood fibers and glue with a photo appliqué (not waterproof). Vinyl is another common type of hard flooring made of synthetic materials and although waterproof, you don't need a soaking wet mop. Make sure you're using a mop that is damp (not sopping wet) to avoid damage.
- Using a spin mop is my preference, although a microfiber flathead or string mop you can easily wring out will work as well. Mop your way out of the room using an "S" pattern and to avoid streaks, always mop with the grain of your floor, keeping the bucket behind you as you go.
- Clean with plain old dish soap and water. I said what I said! We have been bombarded with cleaning solutions and products for floors since we started pulling out the shag and putting in hardwood. As hardwood became more and more popular, so did chemicals and cleaners. Hardwood is beautiful and timeless (if we take care of it) and now it's everywhere, including germ factories like our kitchens and bathrooms.

  o Entire floors: A few drops of Dawn in a bucket of water.
  o Spot-cleaning: Sprinkle baking soda on the spot and scrub with a sponge or try a Magic Eraser. Rinse with warm water and dry, dry, dry.
  o Scuffs: Rub a tennis ball on the scuffs until they're gone or try a Magic Eraser.

- I don't recommend using steam-cleaning mops or similar machines on hardwood. Because wood is porous, it can easily absorb moisture. Steam mops will leave excessive water on the wood and heat the floor, which can lead to swelling, warping, cupping, and eventual damage.

- Avoid ammonia or bleach on hardwood, as it will strip away the finish. I also don't recommend using a vinegar/water mix on your floors for the same reason—save the vinegar for your appliances and other surfaces.
- Skip the wood-rejuvenator products, as they leave residue on your floors. (Please take a moment to think back to my dad and the flying bowl of ice cream.) They may look good at first, but they'll be slippery until they become dull, waxy, greasy, sticky, and/or oily over time (gross).
- Don't forget to read the manufacturer's recommendations to see if your floor requires specialty cleaning products. If your floor is already finished with a hard wax or penetrating oil finish, it requires special manufacturer-approved cleaners that condition and restore the oil finish. But: Using these on a regular urethane-coated floor will cause a hazy, foggy buildup that's hard to remove.

WHAT IF YOU CLEAN YOUR FLOORS REGULARLY BUT YOUR SOCKS LOOK DIRTY AFTER YOU WALK ON THEM?

You've got one of three problems: You're either using a dirty mop, you're not mopping until the water runs clear, or you could possibly be using too much soap or cleaning products on your floors. A few drops of Dawn dish soap or a cleaner of your choice in a bucket of water will suffice. If you use too much cleaner, it can *attract* dirt. So, if a day of walking barefoot in your home equals sooty soles, make sure you're doing those three things. **Clean mop, clear water, and very little product** and your floors (and feet) should be sparkling.

Carpet . . . It Doesn't Matter If It Matches the Drapes

If you have carpets or rugs, you should be vacuuming them at least once a week (more often if you have pets). Like most things, if you do this regularly as a keep-up, it'll make your life easier in the long run. But life happens and so do accidents—you spill a glass of wine when you're a little tipsy or your dog has what I like to call a mistake wee— and these things require spot or stain removal. First, you will need to figure out whether your carpet is made of synthetic or natural fibers.

- Synthetic fibers are those not found in nature; they are made from various chemical compounds. Synthetic fibers most commonly used in carpeting are nylon, polyester, olefin, and triexta.
- Natural fibers are made up of materials that are found in nature. Natural fibers most commonly used in carpeting are wool, sisal, cotton, seagrass, and jute.

There are a lot of supposed "wonder products" out there to clean carpets, but I find it much easier to make my own. These are my go-to four types of carpet cleaners. If you can quickly make all four of these, you'll be ready for every type of carpet stain that comes your way.

Detergent

This is just dish soap and warm water.

- For synthetic carpets: Mix ¼ teaspoon Dawn dish soap with 1 cup warm water.
- For natural-fiber carpets: Mix 1 teaspoon Dawn dish soap with 1 cup warm water.

Vinegar

- For synthetic carpets: Mix ½ cup distilled white vinegar with 1 cup water.
- For natural-fiber carpets: Mix ½ cup distilled white vinegar with ½ cup water.

Solvent

- Nonacetone nail polish remover (can be used on both types of carpets)
- WD-40

How to Remove Stains from Carpets

Stain Group No. 1: Wine (aka why is it always the red)

- Place a clean cloth on the stain to absorb the bulk of the wine.
- Pour the vinegar mixture directly onto the stain.
- Place a clean cloth on top and apply a hot iron to the cloth. The heat will draw the stain into the cloth.
- Repeat that two to three times until the stain has faded, each time with a new clean cloth.
- Once the stain is dry, apply hydrogen peroxide and allow it to completely air dry. Once dry, if the stain is still visible, apply more hydrogen peroxide.

Stain Group No. 2: Most stains (aka dammit stains)

Ketchup, chocolate, coffee, tea, tomato sauce, berries, soda, Gatorade, Kool-Aid (or other dye-heavy fruit drink), butter, salad dressing, cooking oil, crayon, makeup, and nail polish

- Place a clean cloth over the stain and lay something heavy on top for several minutes to absorb as much as you can or just old-school blot the damn thing.
- If you have a synthetic carpet: Dip a white cloth or paper towel into the detergent cleaner for synthetic carpets and dab repeatedly. Let it sit for 15 minutes to allow the cleaner to break down the stain. Take a new dry cloth and soak up the remaining liquid. Next you will want to make sure that cleaner is out of the carpet. Just blot with a cloth soaked in plain warm water and let the area dry completely. Repeat if necessary, until the stain is gone.

- If you have a natural-fiber carpet: Spray the stain with detergent cleaner or the vinegar cleaner and blot with a dry white cloth. Next you will want to make sure that cleaner is out of the carpet. Just spray with plain warm water and blot with a clean dry cloth. Allow the area to dry completely. Repeat if necessary, until the stain is gone.

Stain Group No. 3: Gum and wax
(aka no-more-gum-or-candles-allowed-in-this-house stains)

- For both types of carpet, fill a plastic sandwich bag with ice and either let it sit on the area or rub the bag over the area until the stain hardens.
- Chip at the area with a butter knife or a spatula and vacuum up the pieces.
- Next apply a small amount of solvent with a white cloth and blot the area.
- Rinse by blotting with a clean cloth soaked in plain warm water.

Stain Group No. 4: Ink and marker (aka whyyyyyyyyyy stains)

- For synthetic carpet: Apply a small amount of solvent to a white cloth and blot the area. Wait 10 minutes to dry and repeat if necessary. Rinse by blotting with a cloth soaked in plain warm water and let the area dry completely.
- For natural-fiber carpet: Spray the stain with detergent cleaner or vinegar cleaner and blot with a dry white cloth. Next you will want to make sure that cleaner is out of the carpet. Just spray with plain warm water and blot with a clean dry cloth. Allow the area to dry completely. Repeat if necessary, until the stain is gone. If that doesn't work, you can also spray WD-40 onto the ink stain to soften the ink. Using a clean white cloth, blot the area but do not scrub! Continue blotting the stain until the ink disappears. Allow the area to dry completely. Repeat if necessary, until the stain is gone.

**Stain Group No. 5: Pet accidents
(aka whose-turn-was-it-to-walk-the-dog stains)**

- For synthetic carpet: Dip a white cloth into detergent cleaner and dab. Wait 15 minutes and soak up the excess liquid with a dry white cloth. Next dip the cloth into the vinegar cleaner for synthetic-fiber carpets and dab. Wait until the carpet dries completely. Rinse by blotting with a cloth soaked in plain warm water and let the area dry completely. Repeat if necessary, until the stain is gone.
- For natural-fiber carpet: Spray the stain with the detergent cleaner and blot with a dry white cloth. Next spray the stain with vinegar cleaner and blot with a dry white cloth. Reapply the detergent solution, then blot with a dry white cloth. Rinse by blotting with a cloth soaked in plain warm water and let the area dry completely.

SPECIALTY CLEANING

We've talked a lot about big cleans and little cleans and now I'm going to introduce you to specialty cleaning. These are those every-so-often cleans that are bigger than a big clean. You do them as needed, not on a regular schedule. That's what makes them special!

For my nan, every few months was floor-polishing day. That was the day she pulled out the old General Electric deluxe all-purpose chrome floor polisher with the avocado green splash guard and extra-long cord that conveniently and compactly attached to the handle for easy storage. Like many of her things, she always kept it in its original box. I can remember that box like a photo burned into my brain. She used a paste wax and that GE deluxe turned those floors into an ice rink. They were as slippery as the item descriptions on *Wish*. If our family was visiting my nan, it was the duty of the first person in the door to survey the level of shine and warn the rest of us to brace ourselves. The best approach was to assume an athletic stance at all times,

maintaining your feet shoulder width apart. It was always good practice to hang on to any solid object as a stability aid while navigating
around the house. One moment of dropping your guard and you
would be into an improv break dance. My nan would give each kid a
kiss and a crisp $10 bill when we were leaving . . . I always thought she
was so kind and generous but now I know it was just danger pay for
the visit. Polishing the floors was my nan's favorite specialty clean.

A specialty clean may seem like an enormous undertaking, but the
beauty of it is you get to choose when you do it. It doesn't have to be
scheduled, it's just when you have time or the motivation. The week
before Christmas or the day before your vacation to Mexico is probably not the time for a specialty clean.

Sanitizing the Mattress

First, I *highly* recommend using a mattress cover as a barrier against
dirt, sweat, and stains. Wash it about once per month. It's a lot easier
than having to clean the mattress regularly.

If you have a foam mattress topper, mix equal parts vinegar and
water and spray it on any stains. Soak up all remaining moisture using
a cloth. Sprinkle baking soda on the surface of the mattress topper
and let sit for a few hours. Vacuum the remaining baking soda for a
fresh mattress topper.

Vacuum the mattress for dust mites every 3 to 6 months. If someone in your home has allergies, vacuum more frequently to minimize

dust and other allergens. I also recommend flipping the mattress once every 6 months unless you have a pillowtop mattress, in which case turn it 180 degrees every 6 months.

To spot-clean a mattress, combine a bit of dish soap, baking soda, and a splash of water in a bowl to make a paste, then blot or rub it on with a clean cloth. To deodorize, sprinkle baking soda over the entire surface of the mattress and let it sit for a few hours. (If you do this after you spot-clean, it will also absorb any residual liquid from the spot-cleaning.) Then simply vacuum off the baking soda. For blood or significant sweat stains, use some hydrogen peroxide to cover the stain. Allow it to sit for 15 to 30 minutes, then wipe with a clean cloth. Repeat if necessary until the stain is removed.

Deep-Cleaning the Carpet

We have already covered regular spot-cleaning of your carpets but they also need a specialty clean every 6 months to 1 year depending on foot traffic and use. Maybe your living room is your dining room and you find yourself eating dinner in there more often that you'd like to admit (*me putting my hand up*: guilty). To deep-clean carpet and upholstery, rent or purchase a carpet and upholstery cleaner. Yes, the ones you see at your local supermarket or hardware store and you wonder who actually rents those. Well, you will soon be one of those people. A carpet-and-upholstery cleaner uses water and detergent to deep-clean your carpet. Think of it like a shampoo and rinse for your carpet. I can't give you specific instructions on what to do once you've actually done the renting as they will all be different, but luckily, they come with their own handy-dandy guide. Give it a try, I think you'll find it more fun than you think.

Defrosting the Freezer

You should aim to defrost your freezer at least once a year or more frequently if your freezer is prone to ice buildup. This is also an opportunity to get rid of those freezer burnt chicken nuggets or that mystery sauce you put in a container and never used. Whenever you open your freezer, outside air enters the freezer and allows heat and moisture in. This moisture turns to frost and builds up over time. If your freezer doesn't have an auto defrost option, this frost can become ice that covers the interior air vents and temperature sensors. This can cause your freezer to be less efficient over time and increases ice buildup. Issues with door seals can be the cause of frost buildup as well.

Defrosting a freezer is not a difficult task, but it will take time. You need to wait for the ice to melt in order to do the job.

1. Unplug or turn off your freezer.
2. Remove all the food from your freezer and place it in coolers to keep it from thawing.
3. Lay towels on the floor in front of your freezer and on the shelves to absorb more moisture.
4. Some freezers have a drainage hose to assist with removing water. If your freezer has one, place the end in a bucket.
5. Leave the door open and let the ice melt on its own. If you want to speed up the melting process, you can put a fan near your freezer to help it defrost. Open the freezer door and position the fan so that air circulates into the freezer. The room temperature air will help the ice melt slightly faster.
6. As the ice in your freezer melts, absorb it with towels or a mop.
7. Once all the ice is melted you can start cleaning the inside of your freezer. Mix one tablespoon of baking soda with four cups of hot water, then use a cloth to wipe down the racks, inner walls and door of your freezer. After that, use a cloth to dry everything.

Pro Hack: Once it's clean, spray some cooking spray on the interior walls and base. Wait for approximately 5 minutes, wipe it out, and it will drastically reduce the amount of future frost buildup.

Hacking Away at Hard Water

First: How do you know if you have hard water? Telltale signs include that white crusty stuff around faucets, shower heads, or coffee makers. They need to be descaled occasionally. Perhaps you have a luxurious rain shower head and suddenly the water is only coming out of three holes, one spits out to the left, one to the right, and how you're managing to rinse out your shampoo under the remaining steam is nothing short of a miracle. You most likely have hard water, and the buildup of calcium deposits is blocking the holes.

The key to getting rid of hard-water deposits is vinegar. If you have calcium buildup on taps and faucets from hard water, grab a sandwich bag and fill it with distilled white vinegar. Put the bag of vinegar over the faucet and secure it with rubber bands. Make sure there's enough vinegar in the bag to cover the crusty part of the faucet completely. Then just let it sit for anywhere from 15 to 30 minutes.

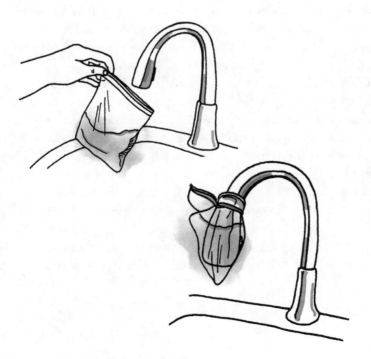

Check intermittently to see if the scale is gone. Always spot test on black fixtures first in an inconspicuous spot. Vinegar will also clean the calcium buildup in your kettle. Just pour a cup of vinegar in the kettle, boil it, dump it, rinse, and it will be as good as new—and your tea will taste like tea again.

Sprucing Up Tile Grout

Grout is the hard stuff between your tiles (looks more like hard sand, not to be confused with caulk, the rubbery, flexible stuff between tiles and tub, sinks, and countertops). Grout is a mixture of cement and sand. It is porous. It is rough. It is water-resistant, but not waterproof, and it absorbs stains easily. For example, you may notice the grout on tile floors in high-traffic areas is dirtier and darker than less high-traffic areas, like the perimeters.

Dirty, gross-looking tile grout can feel like the final frontier of cleaning—best left for grout experts (a job that doesn't exist but we can pretend does). But I promise that no matter where you are in your cleaning journey, you are 100 percent capable of tackling your tile grout. It's easier than you think! Good news is, if your floors are tile, you're already cleaning the grout while you mop.

If there is a small area of your floors where it's gotten a little grubby, you can spot fix by applying toilet bowl cleaner but don't spread it all over; just apply it to the grout line. Don't dilute it. Let it sit for a few minutes, scrub it with a brush, and then rinse it off. Use a medium-stiff brush. If you use a brush that's too hard (like a wire brush), it'll actually remove the grout. If the brush is too soft (like a toothbrush), that'll be more work. A medium brush is just right.

If your grout is beyond a mop or a spot clean, which you will notice as it may look drastically different from its former glory, it's probably time for a commercial grout cleaner. Read and follow the directions and you'll be amazed with the results. You did it!

Keeping Your Caulk Clean

I know, it's chapter two and I haven't even whipped out my caulk yet. Don't worry, there is a lot of caulk talk in this book, but here we're just going to talk about cleaning it. Nobody likes dirty caulk! As I mentioned earlier, caulk is the rubbery, flexible stuff in the space where the tiles meet the tub, sink, or countertop. If you knew anything about me before you bought this book, you already know I love talking about caulk (and if you didn't know that about me yet, boy are you in for a treat).

If there is visible mold or a particularly heavy buildup of mildew on the caulk, it's time to call in the bleach. Here's how I tackle moldy/mildewy caulk, aka dirty caulk:

1. Create a solution of 3 parts water to 1 part bleach.
2. Make sure the area you're working in is well ventilated. Turn on a fan or open a window.
3. Using rubber gloves, eye protection, and a mask is advised. Cover or remove all the towels, bathmats, curtains, and clothing in the room to prevent bleach damage.
4. Grab a brush. Apply the solution and allow it to sit on the caulk for 10 to 15 minutes before scrubbing and rinsing.

Bleach is a great disinfectant that's super effective at removing mold and mildew, but, as I said earlier, it's also quite strong, corrosive, and can irritate or burn skin and eyes. You can use Borax instead (for grout, too) to get a gentler clean (Borax, not to be confused with boric acid, is a combo of boron, sodium, and oxygen):

1. Mix ½ cup Borax with 1 cup warm/hot water in bottle.
2. Shake the mixture until dissolved and apply directly to the area.
3. Dry with a cloth or allow to air-dry.
4. Don't rinse. The Borax will prevent the mold and mildew from coming back.

THINGS YOU DIDN'T KNOW YOU COULD CLEAN WITH A PRESSURE WASHER

Who doesn't love the opportunity to use a power tool! Pressing your thumb on the end of your garden hose is good enough for rinsing off light surface dirt and grime, but it's no match for the cleaning power of a pressure washer. A pressure washer is a gas- or electric-powered machine that forces water out through a hose and nozzle at high pressure in order to blast away heavy, built-up dirt, grime, and stains on many different surfaces. Pressure washers are most commonly used for walkways and siding, but they're a great tool for quickly cleaning up almost anything outdoors—you just have to make sure to use the correct pressure level/nozzle. (Start low and get more aggressive as you go.) If you are planning to restain a deck, you will need to pressure-wash it first. Even if you aren't planning to stain it, using a pressure washer on it is a great way to get rid of mold, mildew, and dirt and give it a fresh look. Try using your pressure washer on exterior brick and garage doors (either to freshen up and clean or to prep before painting), patio furniture, lawn mowers, snowblowers, bicycles, boats, trailers, pools, spas, gutters and soffits, flowerpots, fencing, garage floors, steps, gardening tools, trash cans and recycle bins, awnings, birdbaths, asphalt driveways, stone and rocks, concrete, tile or brick patios, and even cars.

Never pressure-wash electrical panels, air conditioners, lead paint, people, animals, plants, or single-pane windows.

Polishing Silver

When I was a kid, one of my chores was to polish the silverware. Little Melissa would sit down with a cloth and my silver polish (my little tin of Silvo—if you know, you know). Then I would rinse them and dry them. It would take me all bloody day. Luckily, Big Melissa has found an easier, faster, and more natural way. Now I know you may not have silver or use it often. I only use it for special family dinners. My nan bought me one single setting a year starting on my sixteenth birthday. . . . She thought my future husband and I would really like them—hehehehehe. If you have silver, cleaning it with aluminum foil is one of the easiest and cheapest methods to get it back to its shiny former self. This is an elbow grease and chemical-free way.

1. Start by placing a sheet of aluminum foil (shiny-side up) in the bottom of a pan, baking sheet, or sink.
2. Place silverware on the foil.
3. Sprinkle with a light layer of baking soda and 1 tablespoon salt.
4. Boil enough water to completely cover the silverware and pour it into the pan, sheet, or sink.
5. Add 1 cup vinegar and allow the silver pieces to sit in the boiling mixture for 10 minutes.
6. Remove the pieces from the pan, rinse with clean water, dry, and buff with a soft cloth.

I bet you didn't realize you had so many questions about cleaning! But here's hoping you now know how simple it can be. Cleaning is just cleaning. It is not a moral indication of your worth as a person, and it is not actually something you can fail at. Next up? Fixing all the malfunctioning doohickies and whatsits around the house.

FIXING, PREVENTING, INSTALLING, and UPGRADING

This Is Where You Strap It On . . . Your Tool Belt?

. . .

THINK OF THIS SECTION AS "THINGS YOU THOUGHT YOU HAD to hire a TaskRabbit to do but you can actually do yourself because you are way more capable than you think and taking care of your home gives you a sense of pride and makes your home feel even more comfortable and peaceful than you thought it could."

Because here's the thing: Almost anything you do is fixable. If you decide to try filling a hole with drywall and it turns out lumpy and bumpy? Just sand it. (I'll tell you how.) If you caulk your bathtub and it turns out crooked, wipe it off and try again. The biggest thing is not to be so afraid that you don't do anything at all. The more you do things, the better you get. You know I'm good with my caulk, but that's taken years of putting it in cracks and holes.

Here's the other thing: I'm only going to teach you how to do things I consider to be reasonable, because there *are* certain things you should hire experts for. They are experts after all—that's their job! But for those who are interested, there are so many tasks that are much easier than they may seem—tasks that you don't need an expert for and that I want to empower you to try doing yourself if you feel inspired to.

If you *do* hire someone to complete a task that's beyond your current ability or comfort level, why not get your money's worth and watch them do it—in a noncreepy way, of course. Ask questions and learn. Unlike magicians, there isn't a secrecy oath to home repair. Most contractors are happy to share their knowledge.

I once volunteered to paint a room at my workplace, with 15-foot ceilings. I couldn't find a ladder tall enough, so I figured why not just stack a couple of tables and then put the ladder on top of that. Not to brag, but I'm pretty athletic and also good at fix-it stuff, so I figured I'd be fine. Guess what happened next. I fell, obviously, because no one should ever, EVER stack a bunch of tables or put a ladder on *top* of something else. I messed up the paint job and my body. I didn't even know my legs stretched that way, and by the next day I realized they didn't. Best part is it also split my pants from zipper to knee so I had to strategically tie my sweatshirt in various ways to stay decent. Anyway, my point is that we all make mistakes and poor decisions. It's just part of the process.

The same way influencer culture can make us feel bad about all our soda cans not being perfectly aligned in our fully stocked fridge, home-improvement shows can make us feel bad that we're not living in show homes decorated in the latest styles and trends. Don't get me wrong, I love those shows and most of us watch for the real estate porn of it all, but those shows can give a false sense of how complicated and costly some home-improvement projects can be. For example, sometimes on those shows they just pop a prep sink into the new island on the other side of the kitchen, along with new hanging lights above, but fail to tell you that changes like that require major plumbing, electrical, and possibly structural work, yet somehow they managed to do it all for under $1,000 in 30 minutes. Might be slightly unrealistic, to say the least.

My goal is to walk you through the steps so you can feel more capable and confident doing tasks around the house. I want to make your life easier, after all, but most important, I want you to know that perfection isn't really the goal or aim here. Maybe you've only ever used a butter knife to screw in a screw or a rolling pin to hammer in a nail. Maybe you've never seen the value in owning a tool kit or couldn't possibly conceive of using a drill. You know what? SO WHAT? I want to inspire you to take on a project of your own, with actual real tools. If all this section does is give you the confidence the next time your dinner-party conversation gravitates toward your last visit to the home-improvement store (side note: please find more interesting friends if this happens often at dinner parties), then my job here is done.

This chapter has what I consider to be the most common home-improvement, repair, installation, or upgrade chores. They do not require any sort of expertise and will not put you at any sort of health or safety risk. The most important thing to keep in mind, which applies to all tasks, is to read the instructions, gather your tools, think the process through, and have a plan. Even I have to do this, and I'm pretty confident when taking on home improvements. Follow my directions, but always, always, always read the instructions of the tools and accessories you're working with.

HOW TO CHANGE A SHOWER HEAD

Shower heads aren't your great-grandmother's antique dresser—they're like most things these days (I know this makes me sound old): not made to last forever.

There is no rule of thumb for how often you should change your shower head. It depends on whether you have hard water, whether you've just moved into a place and find the idea of using someone else's shower head gross, whether you're just ready for something new . . . Maybe you've cleaned your shower head (see my section on cleaning shower heads and faucets on page 67) and tightened it as much as you can and it's still doling out water in a slow trickle. (Make sure this isn't a water pressure issue first, though—something to ask your landlord, home association, or water company.) Maybe you just want something that better matches your aesthetic. We spend a lot of time in our showers. It's okay to want nice things in there.

The first step is choosing your new shower head. They come in standard sizes, so you shouldn't have to worry about measuring. But in terms of style, be realistic, and keep in mind what we've already gone over about function over form: A rain shower head might look pretty, but if you have low pressure in your house, you're not going to get the desired effect, and it's not going to work the way you expect it to.

TOOLBOX

- Pipe wrench or smooth jaw pliers
- Plumbers tape
- New shower head
- Cloth

THIS IS HOW WE DO IT

1. Unscrew your current shower head using a pipe wrench or smooth jaw pliers by squeezing and turning at the same time (it might be easier to hold the arm pipe in one hand while turning with the other). Leave everything else where it is, including the arm pipe and the flange (the circular cover that goes over the hole in the wall to hide it).

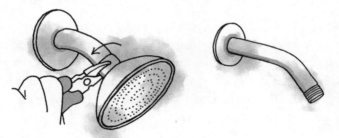

2. Remove any existing plumbers tape that is on the arm pipe (it'll be white).
3. Apply new plumbers tape onto the arm pipe threads. (Threads are the grooves at the end of the arm pipe.

Here's how to think about it: There is no screwing on a nail, but there is threading on a screw. It's the screwy part.) It creates a tighter seal.

4. Install the new shower head by screwing it into the arm pipe and tightening with the pipe wrench or pliers. Wrap a cloth around it (between the pipe and wrench) so the wrench doesn't scratch your new shower head.

5. Turn on the shower and test for leaks.

6. Tighten if necessary, but be careful not to overtighten as this could crack the shower head fitting and make the whole thing loose. Stop tightening just before you feel ready to.

SWITCHING OUT YOUR FAUCETS

Just as with a shower head, changing your faucet or tap is a quick way to make what's old feel new again. Below I'll outline how to take out your old ones. To install the new ones, read the instructions and just work in reverse. Pay close attention as you deinstall—it'll help you keep track of the order of things when you're putting in the new accessories.

TOOLBOX

- Towel
- Adjustable wrench
- New faucet or tap

THIS IS HOW WE DO IT

1. Start by removing any items from under the sink to ensure you have clear access to the area. Putting a towel down underneath whatever you're undoing/disconnecting (e.g., under the counter, on the floor, etc.) is a good idea because there will be some water leakage that you will want to absorb in order to avoid any damage.

2. Turn off the water supply. To turn off the water supply, you need to locate the valve shutoff under the sink. Turn the valve or knob to the right until you can't anymore and/or don't hear running water. Try running the water to check if it's off completely. If your system doesn't have shutoff valves under the sink, you will need to turn off the water supply from the main shutoff. (It's wherever your hot water tank is. For me, that's the basement. For you, it could be somewhere else. It's like a fuse box in that way— you need to know where the one in your home is. If you live somewhere warm, it could be on the outside of the house.) Once you have ensured that the water is off, you can get started.

3. Locate the supply lines that run from the faucet down to the hot and cold valves so that you can disconnect them. They're usually silver braided hoses, whether your plumbing is copper or plastic. (Change these once a decade or risk leaks.) Each supply line (there are usually two: one hot and one cold) is connected to the corresponding valve by a threaded nut. (First balls, then caulk, and now nuts?) You will need to use an adjustable wrench to remove each nut by turning it counterclockwise (lefty

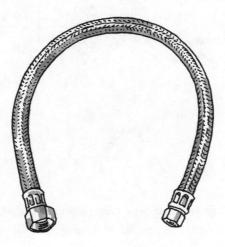

loosey, righty tighty). It is a good idea to secure the water pipe with one hand while you loosen the supply lines with the other until they are completely disconnected.

4.   Loosen the nut that keeps the faucet attached to the sink or counter. Hold the faucet firmly to ensure that it doesn't turn or move as you are unscrewing the nut. You can now pull the faucet up and remove it.

5.   Wipe down the area so that it's clean and dry.

HOLES AND CRACKS

Whether you've got a big hole or a small hole, I'm not here to judge. Trust me, I've seen my fair share and no two holes are the same. No matter the size of your hole or length of your crack, you just need the right tools and some practice. Believe me, you don't need someone else to fill your hole, because once you've filled your own hole you'll feel so good.

First, let's get into some words you've probably heard before but may not be completely clear about.

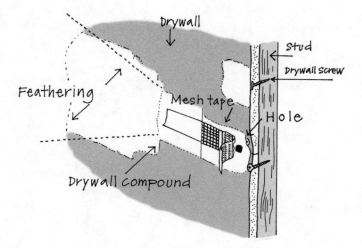

•   Drywall: Drywall comes in large sheets/panels (usually 4 by 8 feet) and it is used in construction to finish interior walls and ceilings. Drywall is attached to the wall studs to create smooth and flat finished walls and ceilings. (Studs are pieces of wood that are basically the bones of your house. Studs are the skeleton; drywall is the skin. When you hear about someone taking their house down to the studs, it means they're bringing it down to the frame of the house and starting from scratch.) Drywall is now commonly used in construction as an alternative to using traditional plaster methods because it's much faster and easier to install. The word "drywall" refers to installation that does not require water, compared to plaster. Finished drywall can be painted within days, whereas plaster walls can take weeks to fully dry. Drywall is durable and requires only simple repairs if damaged. Drywall is made of gypsum (calcium sulfate dihydrate) sandwiched between two layers of thick paper. (Fun fact . . . gypsum is also used to make cement, toothpaste, shampoo, chalk, fertilizer, as well as molds for dinnerware and dental impressions. It was even used to mimic the look of real snow on movie sets once upon a time.)

- Joint compound (aka drywall compound, drywall mud, or just mud): Drywall needs to be finished with something called joint compound at the seams (where the panel edges meet) and over the screw heads. Joint compound can be used for repairs to drywall or plaster.

- Spackle: Spackle is made for small hole, crack, or dent repairs *on* drywall or plaster. It's a little thicker than regular joint compound and doesn't spread as easily, but for small jobs it's great. Spackle is less likely to crack when it dries because it contains special binding agents. This is why it works great for the small jobs.

  o Regular spackle: This has a wet gloppy texture, but on small nail or screw holes you can get away with one coat. Regular spackle can take 1 to 4 hours to dry depending on humidity, thickness of application, and size of hole.

   o Lightweight spackle: This is light and fluffy. It works
      very well on small holes and one coat can be enough.
      Lightweight can dry in as fast as 30 minutes.

Using joint compound is better than spackle for bigger jobs because it comes in larger quantities and is less expensive and much easier to spread than spackle. Joint compound texture is smooth like thick icing. Joint compound has a longer dry time, and because it tends to shrink, it will need multiple coats and sanding in between. Joint compound can take up to 12 to 24 hours to dry.

So first things first, determine the size of your job:

- Holes up to about a ½ inch can be filled with joint compound or spackle.
- Holes between a ½ inch and 5 inches can be repaired with self-adhesive mesh tape and either joint compound or spackle.
- Holes bigger than 5 inches should be repaired with a piece of drywall and joint compound, but should be reinforced with wood. The wood will act as a support for the drywall patch.

The following instructions are for fixing a small hole or crack. For bigger jobs, just apply tape or drywall first and then follow the same steps. (You use the tape to cover the hole, because tape creates a backer/surface/bridge for the compound to adhere to. But even the tape has its limits. If the hole is giant, you need a piece of drywall and wood, or something else more secure.)

TOOLBOX

- Spackle and/or joint compound (aka joint mud, drywall compound, or drywall mud—it differs from place to place; I just call it mud), depending on the size of the job
- Putty or spackle knife
- Self-adhesive mesh tape
- Sandpaper with a sanding block or sanding sponge
- Drywall

THIS IS HOW WE DO IT

(Admit it, you're still singing this line.)

1. Clean or remove any debris from the crack or hole before you begin.
2. Fill the crack or hole with joint compound or spackle using a putty or spackle knife.
3. Apply a thin coat of compound or spackle *over* the entire crack or hole that you just filled. Also apply around the area in order to blend it in. (This is called feathering, and you can read more about it in Put a Feather in Your Cap!, below.) Smooth it with the putty knife as much as possible.
4. Allow the product to dry for the time recommended by the manufacturer. When the area is completely dry, sand the area smooth with sandpaper (be sure to use your sanding block for even pressure, as using sandpaper alone can cause divots from your fingers) or a sanding sponge until smooth. If the repair looks or feels uneven, simply apply another coat and sand again.
5. Wipe away any dust or debris left over from the sanding. It is a good idea to prime the area before painting. Priming will ensure that the finish paint won't absorb through the compound or spackle and show through.

PUT A FEATHER IN YOUR CAP!

Drywall "feathering" is a fancy word for "disguising"! Feathering joint compound or spackle blends the patch into the rest of the wall, so that you don't notice it as much. Adding anything to the wall, no matter how thin a layer, will draw the eye because our eyes gravitate to surface imperfections. So the idea is to reduce the obviousness of the imperfection by creating a "feathered" edge to the patch, blending it into the rest of the wall and fooling the eye. To feather the compound or spackle, you need to apply the compound or spackle to the area around it, wider than just the hole. Gradually make it thinner as you go out. The wider the gradually tapered area on the wall, the less visible the repair will be.

HANGING YOUR SHIT ON THE WALL

Ever encountered one of those frames that has the two little hooks or holes on the back and wondered how in the hell you're supposed to know where to put the nails in the wall to make sure they're the exact same distance as those hooks? Ever banged twelve different holes into the wall attempting and failing to estimate? I have a hack for that, and it doesn't just work for pictures, it works for anything with little hooks or holes on the back that need to hang just so.

TOOLBOX

- Painters' tape/masking tape
- Sharpie/marker
- Level
- Nails/screws
- Hammer
- Anchors (if needed)

THIS IS HOW WE DO IT

1. Place a piece of painters' tape or masking tape on the back of the frame or whatever you want to hang, covering both holes or hangers that are on the frame.

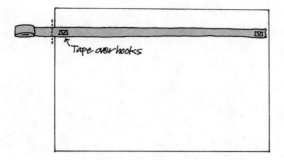

Tape over hooks

2. Mark with a Sharpie on the tape the exact location of the hangers or holes.

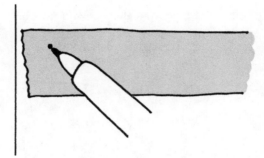

3. Now remove that tape from the frame and stick it on the wall where you want the frame to be. You can use a level against the tape to make sure it will hang straight and now you have created a template for the exact location of where your nail or screw will eventually go.

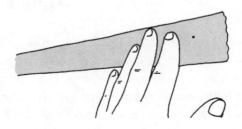

4. Using your template, take the nail or screw where the holes are marked on the tape and use it to puncture a small hole into the wall. This is known as a pilot hole.

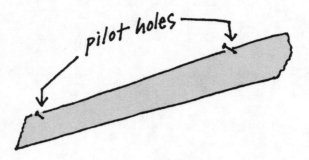

5. Remove the tape from the wall and now hammer in the nails or screw and anchor into the pilot holes. Now you can hang your shit up.

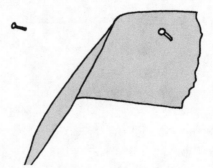

HOW TO GET TURNED ON . . .
BY CHANGING A LIGHT FIXTURE

Besides painting, the easiest way to update or change the look of a room is by changing the light fixtures (by which I mean a sconce, chandelier, or any other light-giving accessory that needs installation). Note that I said "*change* a light fixture" not "*install* a light fixture in a part of the room where there isn't already one." That's because the easiest place to make an electrical switcheroo is where electricity already exists.

The main thing is to make sure that the lighting fixture you're buying is approved for the country where you're installing it. If you buy something online, keep in mind that the sizes of electrical boxes can vary and the electrical standards differ from country to country. Most electricians won't install fixtures that don't meet local standards. For safety reasons, the fixture needs to be approved (any hardware store local to you will sell those).

TOOLBOX

- Knowledge of where your electrical panel is
- Circuit tester (optional)
- Screwdriver
- New light fixture
- Stepladder (if the light fixture is on the ceiling)

THIS IS HOW WE DO IT

1. IT CAN BE SHOCKING! Before messing with anything electrical, you need to turn off the power. Check your electrical panel and locate the circuit breaker control for the room or fixture where you will be working. Switch the circuit to the off position. If you are super keen and happen to have one, you can also use a circuit tester to make sure the power is off. Keep the wall switch of the fixture in the off position until the end of the install. If the circuits in your panel aren't labeled, you can easily figure out which one you're looking for by turning on the light you're looking to replace, then turning off the power to each circuit until the light goes out. Another trick you can do if you're on your own is to turn on a radio that will turn off when the power is off. Having a helper yell out when it's off is much easier. Use a headlamp or flash-

light while you work to avoid fumbling around in the dark.

2. Next you will need to remove the canopy cover to expose the wiring and fixture hardware. The canopy cover is the round covering that sits flush against the ceiling or wall and hides the wiring and mounting hardware. There is usually a screw- or bolt-looking thing holding the canopy in place. Use your screwdriver to undo it and set the canopy aside.

3. You should now see three wires (black, white, and green—or copper) that need to be disconnected in order to completely remove the old fixture. Unscrew the wire connectors (plastic thimble–looking things)—lefty loosey!—and once you've untwisted the wire connectors you can separate the fixture wiring from the ceiling wiring.

4. Basically when you're installing a light fixture, you're connecting three wires from the fixture to three wires that are already installed in the ceiling (with wire connectors), then mounting the fixture and hardware. That's it! The wires are color-coded so that you can't get it wrong: Black goes to black, white goes to white, and the grounding wires (which will either be copper or green) go together. Almost all light fixtures have a universally sized, prewired box in the ceiling, which the three electrical wires come out of. There will be mounting hardware for that that comes with your new light, usually a single metal bar or circular plate. At this point, you're super close, so just refer to the manufacturer's instructions for the specifics for installation.

How to Set the Mood and Choose the Right Bulb

Lightbulbs are something we all need and use, and there are *loads* of options these days. So how many people does it take to figure out what kind of lightbulb to screw in? Lucky for you, just one: me! The main thing to think about when choosing a bulb is: What will you be using the light for? Reading? General illumination? Ambiance? If you have dimmers, check information on the product packaging to ensure that the bulbs you choose are dimmable.

Types of Bulbs

There are four main types of lightbulbs that are commonly used in homes:

Incandescent bulbs

Incandescent bulbs are the traditional, filament lightbulbs that most of us used until about 2012. Incandescent bulbs have a short life span and are not energy efficient. The reason they are less efficient than newer bulbs is because most of the energy they use is turned into heat instead of light, which costs you more on your electric bill and aren't the most eco-friendly.

Fluorescent bulbs

These are usually tubular in shape. They are more energy efficient than incandescent bulbs and have a longer life span. The drawbacks to fluorescent bulbs are that they have what some describe as a delay. They take time to warm up to their full brightness. They also contain mercury, which means they can't be easily disposed of.

Halogen bulbs

Halogen bulbs are a type of filament-style bulb, similar to incandescent bulbs. They are only slightly more energy efficient than incandescent bulbs but can last 1 to 3 years. They can be dangerous to touch when on because they emit a lot of heat.

Light-emitting diode bulbs (LEDs)

LEDs are the most energy-efficient bulbs available. LED bulbs can last up to twenty years and are available in many styles. LED bulbs are more expensive compared to others but because of their long life span and low energy use, they are the more budget-friendly choice overall.

Light Aesthetics and Functionality

When people describe the appearance of light as "warm," "cool," or "daylight," they're referring to the bulbs' lumen output, which will result in a different look and feel.

- Soft white/warm white: These have a yellowish tone that feels more soft, cozy, and relaxing. These are a good option for bedrooms, living rooms, and other areas that you want the lighting to feel softer and less intense.
- Cool white/bright white: These sit outside the yellowish tones but are not quite into the blue tones. Cool white lighting gives off a bright white light that makes for a more neutral atmosphere. These are a good option for kitchens, bathrooms, home offices, or anywhere you want light that is bright but not harsh.
- Daylight: This light has a bright, crisp, bluish tone. Daylight light focuses more on colors and details. These are a good option for reading, home offices, craft rooms and workshops, and accent lighting.

Wattage and Lumens

You're going to be a regular Thomas Edison in no time now. Two things to consider when deciding what lightbulb is best for you are watts and lumens. A lightbulb's wattage tells you how much energy it uses (lower wattage will mean a lower energy bill). Lumens tell you the lightbulb's brightness (higher lumens will be a brighter light). Prior to 2012, almost all lightbulbs were incandescent. Back then you really only had to look at watts. As incandescent bulbs started to be phased out in order to make room for the more energy-efficient ones, packaging started listing wattage equivalent numbers (as a reference to compare to your old incandescent bulb), lumens, energy use and cost, bulb life span, light temperature, and wattage.

LET'S GET CAULKING

If I was ever to have a specialty, it's definitely caulk. No one appreciates good caulk as much as me. Since I can't show you my caulk, let me describe it to you here. Caulk is the rubbery, flexible stuff that seals the joint/gap where your tile/wall meets the tub, sink, or countertop and that stops water from penetrating the joint. It's not just a water barrier, it can be an air barrier or just for aesthetics. It's also the gap filler be-

tween your baseboard and your wall, or on your window and door casing. Caulk is everywhere. I bet you didn't know you were surrounded by so much caulk. Go take a peek: Is the caulk in your shower pristine and smooth or do you have dirty, cracked, crusty, hard caulk? Contrary to popular belief, caulk shouldn't be hard. Nobody likes old, hard, and cracked caulk! If your caulk is looking bad, it's time to replace it, and I mean now, because the longer you wait, the more water damage you risk: Caulk is the barrier between water and wall (whether this is in the tub, the shower, or the kitchen sink), and without it, you're looking at expensive repairs. I won't lie: Removing and replacing caulking is painstaking, but remember that new caulk can be pretty satisfying. Here's what to know about caulk before you get started.

Not all caulk is created equal. It's important to choose the caulk that's right for the area you're putting it in. There are two main types of caulk, acrylic latex and silicone. Acrylic latex is a sealant used for making joints airtight and gap-free. Silicone is a sealant for making joints watertight. Time for caulk talk!

Acrylic Latex Caulk

- Is paintable
- Dries much faster and harder than silicone but shrinks over time and will require more frequent reapplications
- Is less flexible and adaptable to movement than silicone
- Is best for filling gaps, cracks, and holes in interior applications, like between a baseboard and a wall, not anywhere prone to water or extreme temperatures
- Easy to work with and can be smoothed on during application with a wet finger (hehehe)
- Cleans up easy with soap and water

Silicone Caulk

- Is ideal for areas with higher moisture levels, like kitchens, bathrooms, windows, and doors, because of its water resistance. If you're caulking in any areas that will get wet, make sure you're using a caulk that's 100 percent silicone, not just made *with* silicone.

- Is much more flexible than latex when dry, meaning its less likely to crack or split in areas with possible expansion and contraction
- Adheres well to almost any smooth surface
- Is good for larger gaps, cracks, and holes
- Good for exterior use as it can withstand extreme temperatures
- Can't be painted but is available in different colors including clear
- Can't be smoothed with water
- Can bind or hold two materials together unlike latex caulk

TOOLBOX

- Utility knife
- Needle-nose pliers
- Rubbing alcohol (if removing silicone)
- Latex or silicone caulk
- Caulking gun
- Screwdriver or nail (optional)
- Painters' tape/masking tape
- Foaming commercial window cleaner
- Rag

THIS IS HOW WE DO IT

Getting Rid of Old Caulk

1. If you're removing caulk in a bathtub, shower, or sink, cover the drain to make sure none of the old caulking ends up going down the drain.
2. Use the utility knife to cut away the old caulk. If you're working around a tub or a sink be careful not to scratch.

3. Use the needle-nose pliers to pull off the pieces of caulk. It'll take a while, so be patient.

4. As tempting as it may be to leave some bits that are hard to get, you really need to remove all the old caulk to have the best results when recaulking.

5. Clean the area thoroughly. If removing silicone, you will need to clean the area with rubbing alcohol and allow it to dry completely before reapplying.

Putting on New Caulk

For both types of caulk, follow Steps 1 to 7:

1. Make sure the area you are wanting to caulk is clean and dry. Clear of all dirt, dust, grease, or debris.

2. With the utility knife, cut off the tip of the tube of caulk at a 45-degree angle. If using a cylinder tube for a caulking gun, you'll also need to pierce the inside seal to allow for the caulk to come out of the hole. Most caulking guns have a seal punch on the underside of the gun. It's a thin silver rod that will swivel out. You could also use a screwdriver or nail.

3. If using a caulking gun, place the tube into the caulking gun and squeeze the trigger until the plunger stops.

4. To ensure a no-mess, straight line you might opt to use painters' tape on either side of the area you are wanting to caulk. Just make sure you remove the tape after smoothing, before it dries.

5. Place the tip on the spot where you want to begin caulking. You want to work in one direction, left to right or right to left.

6. Apply gentle pressure to the squeeze tube or to the trigger if using a caulking gun, until the caulk begins to flow. Pull the tube/gun away in the direction you are working, while continuously squeezing the tube/trigger to apply an even bead of caulking to the surface.

7. When you reach the end of your desired area, if you are using a caulking gun, you will need to release the pressure on the trigger and press the tension release button located at the back of the gun to stop the flow of caulk. If using a squeeze tube simply release your grip.

For acrylic latex caulk, also follow these next steps:

8. With a wet finger (dampened with water), lightly and slowly smooth the bead of caulk from one end to the other. Wipe the excess caulk onto the rag.
9. Once your caulk looks smooth and even, immediately remove the tape and admire your caulk.

For silicone caulk, also follow these next steps:

8. Spray the bead of caulk with a can of foaming commercial window cleaner.
9. With your finger, slowly smooth the bead of caulk from one end to the other. The window cleaner will stop the silicone from sticking to your finger, allowing you to smooth it with ease. Wipe the excess caulk onto a rag.
10. Once your caulk looks smooth and even, immediately remove the tape and admire your caulk.

DRAIN STUFF: PREVENT AND FIX CLOGGED DRAINS

We've all been there: The tub is suddenly slow to drain or not draining at all. You shine a light down into the drain to inspect a little. With a scowl and a gag, you dig your fingers into it and pull out heaps and heaps of hair (eww). My wife and I recently did this in our new home and discovered 5 feet of the previous owners' hair (no no), and we know that it was 5 feet because the hair and my wife were about the same height. To prevent this and other nightmare-come-to-life sce-

narios, like an ever-present layer of undrained water every time you step into the bath (eww), make sure that all of your drains—including bathroom sinks—have drain covers that stop anything going down that shouldn't go down, and stop anything creepy-crawling up that shouldn't come up. The best drain covers catch hair and any other objects that you can easily remove with a swipe of your finger. Sometimes, though, we get massive clogs, and you can save yourself an expensive call to the plumber with some simpler-than-you-think remedies.

TOOLBOX

- Drain covers (as a preventive)
- Plunger
- Cloth
- Hair-clog remover tool (like The Drain Weasel)
- Drain snake/auger
- Liquid drain cleaner (like Drano)
- Coat hanger
- Dish soap
- Duct tape

There are several reasons why your drain may be clogged. Hair is an obvious one, but it could also just be a buildup of soap scum. You may not know the exact problem until you start to tackle it. I will teach you several ways to unclog a drain, from simple to aggressive. Start using the simplest method and if that unclogs it, great, if not, move on to the next until the problem is resolved.

- Hot water: Shampoo and soap can cause nasty buildup in a drain. Sometimes it can be as simple as pouring very hot (not boiling) water slowly down the drain. While hot water might not work for all clogs, like a massive buildup of matted hair, the water can dissolve most soaps and shampoos fairly quickly and easily.
- Plunger: A plunger is one of the most common tools used to unclog a drain, depending on the type of clog, as well as the design and size of the drain. Pour some hot water into the drain before using the plunger. Cover the overflow opening (if there is one) with a wet cloth to prevent air from escaping as you work with the plunger. Center the plunger over the drain and apply force to create a strong seal. Move the plunger up and down quickly to clear the clog. Remove the plunger and test the drain.
- Hair clog remover tool: A thin, long flexible plastic rod with multiple spikes or even Velcro on the end that you insert into the drain, moving up and down or turning it before removing. The spikes and Velcro are designed to grab hair in the drain. These work well for bathroom sinks, tubs, and shower drains. The result can be pretty gross, but often fixes a clog within minutes. This will likely become your most-used clog fixer because it cleans up clogs that are located close to the drain within the pipe.
- Drain snake/auger: Another manual tool, this one is a flexible metal cable coiled inside a drum. Drain snakes are best for removing clogs located deeper in the drain system and work on

toilets, kitchen and bath sinks, tubs, and showers. You simply place the metal fusilli/corkscrew-looking end of the cable in the pipe, then turn the drum to extend the cable lower and lower. The corkscrew end is designed to grab the clog and pull it out.

- Liquid drain cleaner: Loosens and dissolves soap scum, hair, grease, and paper. Liquid cleaners work on clogs that aren't too deep. Caution: Make sure the room you are in is well ventilated as liquid drain cleaners are incredibly toxic. It is imperative to follow the specific manufacturer's instructions on the bottle, but generally they work by pouring the solution into the drain, allowing it to work for a specific period of time, and then running the water to test the drain.

TOILET CLOGS

It wasn't me, I swear. How many times have you heard this, or even said it yourself? No one ever takes responsibility for a toilet clog, but it does happen, and with kids, it can happen more often than you think. The easiest and best way to deal with a clogged toilet is with a plunger. If you ever find yourself in a situation where you don't have a plunger, I will teach you several ways to unclog it with items you may already have at home. With a little gumption, you will get your clogged toilet back up and running in no time.

A toilet clog means that your toilet drain is either partially or completely blocked. The most common is a partial blockage (someone used way too much toilet paper). An indicator of a partial blockage would be when the toilet is flushed, the water doesn't rush down and clear the waste. Instead, the water level rises but usually drains down slowly to its normal level within a few minutes. You may not even know the toilet is clogged until you flush it.

- Plunger: Place the plunger directly over the drain hole to create a seal. Make sure there is enough water in the bowl to cover the plunger. Ensure your first plunge is a gentle one. A hard plunge will cause water—and other stuff—to splash out of the toilet onto the floor and, yes, you. A gentle plunge and hold will push out the trapped air, allowing you to now plunge more aggressively in and out while maintaining the seal. This may take ten to fifteen plunges. The plunging action will force water in both directions within the drain, which should effectively clear most common clogs.

- Hot water: Adding hot water may help to move things along. Fill a container with hot but not boiling water. Boiling water could cause a porcelain toilet to crack. Pour the hot water into the toilet from at least waist height. The force of the water from that height could force the obstruction to dislodge and clear the clog.

- Dish soap: Dish soap could be a surprising remedy for a toilet clog. The soap can help to lubricate the clogged drain and allow the obstruction to slide down more easily. Pour ¼ to ½ cup of soap into the toilet. Let it sit for ten to fifteen minutes to allow the soap to work its slippery magic.

- DIY hanger drain snake/auger: This is when those horrible wire hangers from the dry cleaner finally have a use. A more severe blockage could require manually pushing the obstruction. A hanger can be a good option if the obstruction is in the first few inches of the drain. Unravel and straighten the hanger, wrap the end of the wire with duct tape to prevent the sharp end from scratching the porcelain of your toilet. Push one end of the wire into the drain until the obstruction becomes free and flows down the drain.

- Drain snake/auger: This is a flexible metal cable coiled inside a drum. Drain snakes are best for removing clogs located deeper in the drain system and work on toilets, kitchen and bath sinks, tubs, and showers. You simply place the metal fusilli/corkscrew-looking end of the cable in the pipe, then turn the drum to extend the cable deeper into the drain. The corkscrew end is designed to grab the clog and pull it out. As a mom, I have excavated lots of toilet goodies that my kids have flushed. It seemed like it was just yesterday that I was chasing a running toddler through the house begging them not to flush the remote control or car keys while they simply evil-laughed and only ran faster to the toilet.

REPLACING DOORKNOBS AND HANDLES

You might decide to switch out your handles and knobs because they're not working properly anymore, they're corroded, or maybe you just think they're ugly and want a change. It's a relatively wallet-friendly way to make an impactful change on your décor. The best part? Changing them out is easy! Taking the old one out is a bit more difficult than installing the new one, but the great news is that because you're throwing it away, you do not need to be gentle with the old hardware. Just be careful not to damage the door.

TOOLBOX

- New door handle (see below for specifics)
- Screwdriver
- Nail (optional)

First, you need to figure out what type of door handle you have so you can purchase the right one to replace it with. There are basically four different types of door handles.

- Entrance or keyed (used on exterior doors)
- Privacy (used for bathrooms)
- Passage (used for closets and bedroom doors)
- Dummy (just a surface mount handle used on closet doors; they're like passage handles with one major exception: They don't even turn.)

There are also different sizes you need to consider when purchasing a new handle, but you won't know what size you need until you take off the old hardware (see Removing the Old Handle, Step 5 below).

THIS IS HOW WE DO IT

Removing the Old Handle

1. The first thing you need to do in order to remove your door handle is to figure out where the screws are located. If you can see the screws, you are good to remove them; however, many handles are designed to hide the screws for a sleeker look. If this is the case, you may have to look closely and inspect the top, base, and along the sides for an opening. If you see a small pinhole or slot instead of visible screws, you will need to slide the rose (hole cover) back to reveal the screws. To do this, look for a release mechanism slot on the rose that you can put your flat-head screwdriver into to release so that it can be pulled back. Oftentimes the handle will have a small hole that you can stick a nail into, which will release the handle.

2. Hold the inner and outer door handles in place on each side of the door and pull them apart to remove them (put them aside for now).

3. Slide the latching mechanism out of the door once both handles are out.

4. Unscrew and remove the strike plate from the door jamb. (It's the metal plate with a hole in it for the lock bolt.)

5. Check your old latch for a number stamped somewhere on it, either 2-¾ or 2-⅜ inches. This is the doorknob's "backset," which is the distance from the door's edge to the center of the doorknob hole. All standard doorknobs have a backset of either 2-¾ or 2-⅜ inches.

   o You will need to choose a new handle with the same backset distance. If you can't find those numbers or you are unsure, bring your old set to the store when you are purchasing a new one.

Installing the New Handle

1. Insert the new latch into the hole in the door. Be sure to turn it to face the correct direction of the door swing and screw in.
2. Take the two new handles and interlock them with each other through the hole in the door and into the latch.
3. Once the handle is centered over the hole, you can screw it together until it feels tight and secure.
4. Install the new strike plate on the door jamb.
5. Test the new handle, making sure it turns freely. Ensure the latch easily moves in and out by manually pushing it with your fingers several times. Open and close the door several times to make sure it lines up and latches easily.

GET INTO MY "PAINTS"

Of all the jobs in the world, a paint job is perhaps one of the most satisfying. It's so easily DIY and packs a major punch for a relatively minor expense. It can be an absolute game changer if you're looking for a way to update your space. Yes, it takes patience and determination but it's a great starter DIY to build confidence. If you're up for the challenge, painting your own space is an easy way to spiff up your joint and also feel a tremendous sense of accomplishment.

TOOLBOX

- Drop cloths or floor paper
- Primer
- Paint
- Paintbrushes
- Rollers
- Roller cover
- Paint can opener or a flathead screwdriver
- Stir sticks

- Paint roller tray and plastic liner
- Handheld paint pail
- Plastic wrap (for wrapping brushes when needed)
- Paint strainer (or a pair of pantyhose; see Painting Tips and Hacks, page 105)
- Ladder/step stool
- Paint handle extenders (or broom sticks of different lengths; see Painting Tips and Hacks, page 105)
- Spackle knife
- Painters' tape

Choose the Right Brush

Bristle Type

Paintbrushes are available with either synthetic bristles or natural bristles (made from animal hair). For the most part, spending more will provide you with a better quality brush and a better quality finish. If you are using a water-based paint, stain, or varnish, you will want a brush with synthetic bristles. If you are using an oil-based paint, stain, or varnish, you will want a natural bristle.

Size

If you're painting something small or finicky and need more precise control, you will want a small 1-½-inch brush. For wide trim or walls (mostly cutting in), a 2-½-inch brush is perfect (and my favorite). This size is my personal go-to for most jobs. If, however, you are painting siding, fencing, or other wide and flat surfaces, you will want to use a 3-inch brush for quicker and larger area coverage.

Shape

Now that you know what bristles you need and what size you need, the last thing you need to choose is shape. Most brushes are either angled or square-tipped. If you are painting a room, you will need to cut in (we'll get to that) before rolling walls, and for that you will want a brush with an angled tip. The angled tip makes it easier to control the line of paint for a more accurate finish. You would use a square-tipped brush for painting wide or flat surfaces.

Choose the Right Roller Cover

Size

For roller covers, the standard length is 9 inches. For smaller areas, a 4-inch roller is typically used. Bigger rollers and covers are for bigger surfaces like walls and ceilings and smaller rollers and covers are better for doors, furniture, and cabinets.

Nap Height

Choose the nap height based on the surface being painted.

- $\frac{3}{16}$ to $\frac{1}{4}$ inch: For very smooth surfaces like metal doors, smooth wood, and plaster.
- $\frac{3}{8}$ to $\frac{1}{2}$ inch: For smooth and semismooth surfaces like drywall, acoustic tile, paneling, or smooth concrete.
- $\frac{3}{4}$ to 1 inch: For semirough surfaces like wood, lightly textured walls and ceilings, or stucco.
- 1-$\frac{1}{4}$ to 1-$\frac{1}{2}$ inches: For extremely rough or textured surfaces like stucco, textured ceilings, brick, rough wood, or concrete block.

Choose the Right Paint

Oil-Based Paint vs. Water-Based Paint

The difference between oil-based paint and water-based paint is referring to the type of solvent used in the paint, which is the liquid part of the paint that evaporates as the paint dries.

Oil-based paints

- Contain a solvent—typically a mineral turpentine
- Can have a higher sheen level

- Dry harder and hold up well to heavy wear and tear
- Are not flexible and more likely to dry out, split, and crack over time
- Are known to yellow over time
- Have thicker consistency
- Have harmful VOCs (volatile organic content)
- Can only be cleaned up using paint thinner, turpentine, or mineral spirits

Water-based (aka latex) paints

- Use mostly water as their solvent
- Have an overall lower sheen finish but can usually maintain their sheen over a longer period of time
- Dry quite hard and stand up to wear and tear. Water-based paints are more flexible so when they expand and contract with weather, they are less susceptible to cracking.
- Are easier to use, clean up, and are more environmentally friendly
- Have great color retention over time
- Dry faster
- Have lower VOCs
- Can typically be used over existing oil-based paints with prep, but oil-based paints cannot be used over water-based paints.
- Are great on high-traffic areas and will even hold up on stairs and banisters

Choose the Right Sheen

That's easy: Martin! I kid. Sheen indicates how glossy a paint will be when it's dry.

Gloss

- These include satin, pearl, gloss, and semigloss.
- They're shinier and reflect more light.

- They clean easily.
- They show more imperfections on the wall.
- Mostly used on trim, baseboard, molding, stairs, railings, and furniture.

Matte

- These include flat, eggshell, and matte.
- They diffuse the light to make the surface less shiny.
- They are harder to clean without leaving wipe marks.
- They show fewer imperfections than gloss.
- They're great for low-traffic areas or walls with many imperfections.
- The most common sheen is eggshell because it fits comfortably in the middle of the sheen range.

Ceiling Paint

Ceiling paint is heavier and thicker than regular wall paint, making it less likely to drip during the overhead application. It dries much faster and will cover light staining better than regular wall paint will. Most ceiling paint is a matte or flat finish that does not reflect much light, thus hides imperfections, which is great for most ceilings.

In rooms with higher levels of humidity like bathrooms or laundry rooms, or kitchens where food can splatter, some people choose a ceiling paint with sheen for better wipeability. Ceiling paint is made to resist mildew as well as staining from smoke or cooking, whereas regular wall paint is not.

How Much Paint Do I Need?

What did the paint do when it got cold? It put on another coat . . . sorry. Almost every wall needs at least two coats of paint, minimum, if changing the color. Don't be fooled by paint that claims to be one-coat coverage. Depending on the quality of the paint, more than two coats may be needed to achieve your desired color and finish.

As to how much paint you need to paint an area, the general rule of thumb is one gallon is needed for 400 square feet of coverage. To calculate the square footage of your area, multiply the width by the height of each wall or the ceiling in your space. Next, you'll need to calculate the square footage of each window and door, or any other area that will *not* be painted and deduct that from the total. Now, you know your square footage.

PAINTING TIPS AND HACKS

- Invest in a good brush: It will last longer, making it cheaper in the long run, and it yields a better result. No bristles falling off during painting.
- Invest in a good sturdy roller tray and use a plastic liner: Flimsy lightweight trays can tip or move and risk spilling. A plastic liner will save cleanup time (you can even use a plastic bag in a pinch).
- Brush hack: Wrap some painters' tape around the metal base of the brush, where the bristles end. This will stop excess paint from dripping down the handle as you're painting.
- Roller hacks: Before using it, wrap a new roller with painters' tape and pull it off to remove any loose lint so it doesn't end up on your walls. When using water-based paint, dampen your roller with a little water before you start, it will help the roller to absorb the paint.
- Wrap your brush: If you need to take a break while painting, wrap your brush in plastic wrap to prevent it drying out. In a pinch you can use aluminum foil or a plastic bag, just don't let the logo on the bag touch the bristles as it may transfer the dye to your brush. If it's going to be more than a few hours, just wash it.
- Pantyhose make a great paint strainer: For clumpy paint, this is a great and cheaper alternative to a store-bought paint strainer.

- Shake the can by the handle as opposed to holding the can itself. It's easier and you can save yourself the full-body workout for the rolling. This will also reduce the amount of stirring you will need to do.
- "Boxing" paint: If you're coming to the end of one can and about to open a second, it is best to combine a little of the old and the new together. There are many variables from one can to the next, human error, computer error, slight change in formula, etc. This is known as "boxing" paint.
- Consider using an extension pole: The farther you have to reach, the heavier and more painful it can be to do the job. I recommend an adjustable extendable pole. You can also use a broomstick: Simply unscrew the bristle section and screw on your roller. It's a standard fitting, male/female.
- Use your spackle knife to get excess paint off your roller before removing it for cleanup. Paint is expensive, so to minimize waste, take your spackle knife and firmly run it down the edge of the roller to take off any excess paint. You won't believe how much paint the roller can hold.

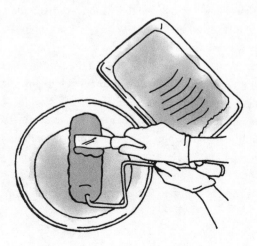

THIS IS HOW WE DO IT

Prepping Your Room for Painting

- Move furniture and other items out of the room. If you can't move furniture out of the room, move it to the center and cover it with drop cloths.
- Cover light fixtures and ceiling fans.
- Remove any outlet covers and vent covers.
- Tape off the edges of areas not to be painted like door trim, baseboards, ceiling, etc. (optional).
- Repair any picture holes or other wall damage (you are now a drywall pro, so you can do this!).
- Clean the walls thoroughly of any dust and dirt using a duster or damp cloth before painting.
- If you're using a not-new can of paint and it seems clumpy, use a paint strainer. It's sometimes hard to know how old paint is because you don't know how long it was sitting around at the store before you bought it. If you open up a can of paint, as long as it's stirrable, you can use it. It's even okay if it smells a little. If it's at all chunky or has a skin, that's when you use a strainer. If it's overly thick or hard, throw it away. It should be like a heavy cream, not like peanut butter.
- Once you have determined your paint is good to go, you are ready to transfer it into your paint tray for rolling or your handheld paint pail for brush work. If you're wondering why you need to transfer your paint to begin with, the answer is simple: Paint cans are heavy! You don't want to lug an entire one up a ladder when you could just bring up a bit at a time. The only time I ever paint out of a can is if it's one-quarter or less full and I know I'm going to use it up.

Priming Is a Fancy Way of
Saying Preparing

What Is Primer?

Primer looks like really boring paint. It's a special undercoat or base paint with an adhesive binder in it. It seals the surface and leaves a smooth and clean area for paint to adhere to. Not every painting project will require priming first.

When Do You Need to Prime?

- You will need to prime your walls before painting if the surface is porous. Brand-new drywall is a very porous material. Both the paper that covers the drywall and the joint compound need to be sealed with primer before you can paint.
- If you have simply patched or made small repairs to drywall with spackle or joint compound on the surface, there is no need to prime. You can take a small amount of your regular paint and lightly brush it on the repaired areas before painting the entire wall.
- If your walls have stains from water damage, smoke, cooking, crayon, or marker, you should prime first so stains won't show through the paint (stain blocking).
- Glossy surfaces are difficult for paint to adhere to. If your walls were previously painted with a high-gloss paint, you will need to prime first.
- Primer will also block and seal in food, pet, and smoke odors and prevent them from returning.
- If you are going from a very dark color to a very light color, it is best to prime first. Dark paint colors will bleed or show through lighter colors, so if you want to save yourself the work of five or six coats of paint and the cost of that paint, priming first is best.

What About Paint and Primer in One?

There are many types of paint on the market with primer already added to the paint. They are known as all-in-one paint and primer or self-priming paints. They are thicker and do provide good coverage. However, they aren't as good as they advertise. Taking the time to prime the surface with a separate primer before painting will yield far better results.

What Is Tinted Primer?

Primers can be tinted to closely match the color of your paint. A tinted primer could reduce the need for multiple coats of paint, especially vibrant colors. Primer is less expensive than paint, so it could lower your painting costs.

May I Cut In?

Although a roller is the best way to apply paint to large surfaces like walls and ceilings, a roller will not get into corners or to the edges/details of trim or molding. For that you will need to use a paintbrush to do something called "cutting in." Cutting in does take some practice and some patience, but with the right paintbrush and a steady hand, you can paint a perfectly straight line. If you don't feel confident or it's your first time, you can always use painters' tape to mask off the areas you don't want painted until you get the hang of it. Using your angled brush, you are going to "cut in" by painting an edge between the ceiling and the walls and along any trim or molding and the corners from top to bottom. You will also use your brush to fill in any small pieces of wall that a regular roller won't fit. Start by dipping the tip of the brush into the paint. Next, either lightly drag the bristles against the edge of the paint pail or lightly tap it against the side of the pail to remove the excess paint. You don't need a lot of paint because you will only be painting a small area at a time. Make sure you are using a sturdy ladder or step stool for higher areas. You want to be just below eye level in order to achieve a straight line. Fill a paint pail with some paint so you won't be up and down the ladder a million times or lugging around a heavy paint can.

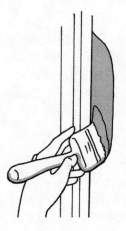

Hold your brush parallel or horizontally to the floor with a loose pencil-like grip. Start by painting about 1 inch away from the area you are cutting in and let the bristles flare or fan out slightly. The outer bristles will be making your line. Slowly paint a 10- to 12-inch strip/line at a time on the wall. Paint the next section into the previous one (overlap) in order to blend them. Watch your line and relax! You actually need to relax because you need to control your breathing while cutting in; huffing and puffing will cause your hand to move. For corners, use a downward stroke. For tight corners, wiggling your brush into the corners will help to get your brush into the area without risking a blob mistake.

Roll with It

The fun part! Pour your paint into the tray with the label facing toward you so that if it drips, you will still be able to read it in the future. You will want to fill the well of the tray halfway full. Dip half of the roller into the well of the paint tray. Bring the roller to the top of the ribbed (for her pleasure) part of the paint tray and back-roll the paint roller back and forth a few times, to evenly disperse the paint over the entire roller. You may need to do this a few times until the roller is completely and evenly covered.

Start working from top to bottom and left to right, rolling up and down across the wall in a series of V- or W-shaped sweeping rolls until the section is covered. Before reloading the roller with paint and before moving on to the next section, roll over or overlap the edge of the area you just finished with a smooth, continuous stroke from top to bottom. These smoothing strokes, called back-rolling, help to blend and cover up lines and roller marks. Reload and keep going. The idea is to work fast enough so that you're always overlapping newly applied paint onto paint that is still wet. If you stop in the middle of a wall and then start painting after the section has dried, a line or mark will be visible where the two areas join. Continue with this technique for the entire room. Depending on the humidity level and air temperature, you will need to wait for 1 to 3 hours for the first coat to dry before applying a second coat or any subsequent coats. Regularly stir or mix your paint to avoid a paint skin from forming. If at any time you leave your paint sitting for a period of time, it should be covered. Even when dry to the touch, most paint will take up to 30 days to completely cure. So, it's important to use caution with newly painted surfaces until they cure and can withstand daily wear and tear.

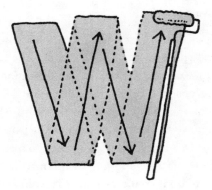

EASY RE-COVER DIY

Are you intrigued by furniture flippers and upcyclers, regular people like you and me slamming on the breaks to pick up curbside furniture trash to transform it into beautiful pieces? Why are they doing this—it seems like a lot of work. Well, the simple answer is that older furniture is typically solid wood and well made compared to most modern furniture. Do you remember the 1977 song by Trooper? Well, I'm pretty sure it was written about the furniture many of us buy today . . . it's made for a good time (not a long time)!

A very easy DIY furniture flip that anyone can do as a starter project is re-covering. New fabric can give furniture a new life. It is super easy to re-cover basic dining chair seats. Maybe you have a chair, or you found an old stool that looks great, and you can see the potential, but the dusty rose and hunter green floral fabric seats are just not your vibe.

TOOLBOX

- Dining chair or stool to reupholster
- Measuring tape
- New fabric
- Screwdriver
- Pair of scissors
- Staple gun (and staples)
- Tape measure

THIS IS HOW WE DO IT

1. Start by measuring the cushion to determine the amount of fabric you will need. Just make sure to allow a few inches all around to wrap under the bottom of the seat.
2. Next, remove the seat from the base. It is usually held to the frame by a few screws. If you need to make any repairs or want to add new padding or refinish the chair, this is the time to do it. You can remove the old fabric from the seat, but you don't have to, you can go right over top of it.
3. Next, purchase some fabric from a fabric store. The ladies in the fabric store will help you. They will figure out very quickly you have no idea and that you may have never been in a fabric store, but they know what they are talking about and can guide you in the direction of the right fabric for your project.

4. Next, cut the fabric to fit each seat. Wrap/stretch it over the seat and use a staple gun (not the one on your desk) to attach it tightly to the seat's underside by stretching it taut and working your way around all sides. Pleat the fabric around the corners before stapling. Then reattach to the base and you have a new old piece of furniture.

NICE DRAWERS

Push your panties to the side, we're about to get busy. Do you have stinky drawers? Don't worry, you're not the only one. It's not you, it's the lack of air circulation in the drawer. There is a way to fix it, an old-school method my mother and my grandmother always used: liners. Liners create a barrier between your clothes and wood. They didn't just use them in their dresser drawers, they used them in kitchen and bathroom cabinets and on shelves. Liners protected surfaces from scratching and damage from stains and spills and made cleanup easier. They also covered up the sins of those who had lived in the home previously. Shelf and drawer liners won't extend the life of your shelves or drawers, but they can keep them looking cleaner and smelling fresher. Modern shelf and drawer liners offer so many choices. This is totally a mini-DIY you can do to spruce things up and protect them.

What Kind of Liner?

All you really need to do is choose the kind of liner you need:

Fabric Liners

These are washable and can be used long-term. They can be difficult for high-traffic drawers and shelves because they slide around and don't stay in place well.

Plastic Liners

These are ideal for open wire shelves, to stop items from wobbling or falling through the open spaces in the shelving.

Foam Liners

These give a little extra padding for delicate or breakable items. They are inexpensive and usually come in sheets or rolls that can easily be cut. To clean them, you have to remove them.

Paper Liners

These are most commonly used in dresser drawers. They often come scented (like in the old days) to keep clothes smelling fresh and help to avoid mustiness, especially with old or antique wood pieces. If you have a rough wood drawer, they will also protect clothing from rubbing and possible snags.

Adhesive Vinyl Roll Liners

These are the least expensive option and are available in the widest variety of colors and patterns. Adhesive liners can be finicky to match and get a seamless look. They leave a sticky residue when removed.

Adhesive Vinyl Tiles

These are my favorite for kitchen and bathroom drawers. You can pick up adhesive vinyl tiles from most hardware stores in many different sizes, colors, and patterns. They can be cut with a utility knife or scissors, and they offer a little extra padding and more substantial protection, especially for bathroom drawers with makeup and toothpaste. They also protect well against utensil scuffs in kitchen drawers. They do, however, leave a sticky residue when removed.

Affordable Liner Alternatives

These can all be cut to size, offer a good temporary fix, and will save you the cost of buying actual liners:

- Wallpaper
- Wax paper
- Stiff fabric
- Wrapping paper
- Cork sheets

- Flexible plastic cutting board
- Placemats

TOOLBOX

- Liner of choice
- Measuring tape
- Utility knife or scissors

THIS IS HOW WE DO IT

Just stick it in (that's what she said?). No, but really—that's it. Just measure and trim to fit if you need to, then lay that baby down.

. . .

So, surprise: You just got organized, cleaned your house, and fixed things along the way. To recap:

- Keep up so you don't have to catch up.
- Be ruthless when organizing your home. Use SMART goals and the Keep, Toss, Donate, Sell strategy.
- Don't use Pledge on the stairs if your dad is walking down them carrying ice cream.
- You don't need a million products to keep a clean home.
- Schedule regular cleaning and tidying to make an insurmountable task surmountable (is that a word?).
- Have a slice of pie every day instead of the whole pie on Saturday.
- You are more capable than you think when it comes to fixing and sprucing things up around your home.
- When asking for caulk at the hardware store, be sure to enunciate the "L" to avoid embarrassment.

2.

This Is Where You
Wish Your
Bank Account
Filled Up as Fast as
Your Laundry Basket

SORTING AND WASHING

This Is Where You
Sort Your Shit Out

. . .

Y OU KNOW IT. I KNOW IT. IT'S THE BIG UGLY MONSTER IN THE corner of the bedroom: the Laundry Chair. The chair that was supposed to be for lounging elegantly with a steaming cup of tea and a good book, leaning on a luxurious accent pillow, a blanket perfectly draped across your lap, along with a very tiny, well-behaved dog who

doesn't shed or bark. Instead, it's where we dump semi dirty clothes that need to be washed after a few more wears, clean clothes that need to be folded, and folded clothes that haven't been put away yet.

The Laundry Chair probably makes you feel stressed out at best, and at worst so anxious you don't even want to look at that corner of your room. When it comes to laundry, we often feel like there's just so much of it, that there must be people living in your home that you haven't met yet. It can feel way too overwhelming to even start.

But here's the thing: Laundry doesn't have to be scary. It doesn't have to be hard. Personally, I love laundry, and it's not because I have some magical genetic predisposition. Yes, a clean white shirt gives me dirty thoughts. You have your kinks, I have mine. But even if you've never fantasized about a freshly laundered pile of T-shirts, I promise, you can be good at doing laundry, too. And the payoff is worth it. Being on top of your laundry is one of the easiest ways to feel in control and accomplished in your home.

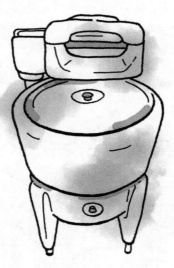

Growing up, my nan's wringer washer was a beast! It had a big basin with a dangerous-looking robin's-egg blue agitator that she manually filled with a hose that my grandfather had rigged up. She would sprinkle in some Tide XK powder and once it was full, she plugged it in and the agitator got to work. It wasn't a whispering machine. It sounded like an 18-wheeler on a bumpy road. She would let the agitator splotch back and forth until she felt the clothes were clean enough. She just knew. Then I stood on my special helper stool while she pulled the soaked clothes out of the basin and fed them through the wringer. There was a so-called safety release just in case your six-year-old finger happened to wander into the wringer (sometimes it did . . . and it hurt!). I guided those pancake-flat clothes out of the other side of the wringer and tossed them into the rinse sink to await the next step. From the rinse sink my nan shook the clothes vigorously through the water, reversed the wringer and sent them though for a second squishing. I tossed them into the hamper and then we hung them on the line to dry. Honing my skills on the old wringer brought me all the way here to teach you everything I know about laundry and the like.

Even before I became TikTok's unofficial Laundry Lesbian (a title I wear with pride), I was never a "Sunday is laundry day" person. It never interested me. For starters, I don't want to spend an entire day out of my weekend doing laundry; plus, what happens if I go away for the weekend and miss the designated laundry day? Then I'm in a tizzy for the rest of the week catching up. To avoid that, I throw in a load after work *every day*, move it to the dryer after dinner, and then put it away quick. It's second nature and doesn't feel like a chore because it's just part of my routine, like brushing my teeth or taking a shower. Having three kids easily provides me with enough laundry for a load every day, but if your situation is different and you don't have enough for a load a day, try doing one every two days or even every third day. Any regular system will lessen the weekend laundry blow.

Keep up instead of catching up. *Keep* up instead of *catching* up. Every time I do my laundry, that's what I'm doing. The benefits of this are: You will always have clean clothes that are ready to wear. It eliminates the last-minute laundry rush to wash what you want or need to wear. There are no piles of laundry in baskets, on furniture, or sitting in the dryer wrinkled waiting for the infamous "one more fluff cycle." No time is wasted digging and looking for that specific item that you can't remember if it's clean or dirty.

I get it. When you're sitting on the couch at the end of a long workday, it feels like you're giving yourself a much-deserved break by not doing the laundry, but that's actually a bit of a trick you're playing on yourself: By letting yourself off the hook tonight, you're making tomorrow much more daunting. Every day you give yourself an out, you are making things harder for yourself later on. So let me say it one more time, let me scream it for the people in the back, the key to laundry is keeping up so you don't have to catch up.

The laundry room or area often ends up as the dumping ground in your home. Yes, I know, you thought we were done with the cleaning chapter, but a tidy laundry area is a more efficient one. Keeping this space free of clutter will actually, believe it or not, make doing laundry more enticing. Having space to easily transfer laundry from one machine to another, space to fold (even if it's just standing in front of the dryer), having easy access to detergents, stain remover, drying racks, and the ironing board will make doing laundry so much easier.

Now, doing laundry every day works for me. I have a wife, three kids, and two dogs, so doing one load every day is the system that works best for us; it's how we keep up. But again, I'm not saying you have to do it every day, but I am telling you, *you* have to keep it up. I'm telling you not to let it get to the point that your laundry day is the day you have nothing to wear but your wedding dress. I want you to find that continuously moving system—whatever works best for your unique situation—to avoid a laundry pileup.

So, let's do it, let's do the fucking laundry. One load at a time. Here we go.

WHEN IT COMES TO SUSTAINABILITY AND THE WASH, YOUR MACHINE IS THE MOST IMPORTANT FACTOR

If you are conscious about the environmental impact of doing daily laundry, the machine you are using will have a considerable effect on the amount of energy and water you use. Older machines tend to use more energy and more water while a newer high-efficiency machine will use less. Newer washing machines not only use less water and energy but the detergent for high-efficiency machines generally works best in colder temperatures while using less of it. Higher spin speeds in newer washers means less time needed in the dryer, which will also save energy. To ensure efficiency in every wash, never fill the machine more than ¾ full. An overloaded machine will not allow the water and detergent to dissolve or clean the clothes. Most newer dryers will have sensors that help detect moisture on clothes, which means it will only run until the clothes are dry instead of for the duration of whatever the timer was set for.

It can be both financially and environmentally beneficial to upgrade machines that are more than 10 years old.

TOOLBOX

Remember: When in doubt, go with your brand loyalties, what's most affordable, or anything else that floats your laundry-loving boat. These are just my preferences:

- Sorting baskets
- Premium liquid detergent (I use Persil or Tide)
- Scent beads
- Oxygenated bleach
- Bookmarks (see Want to Wear Something More Than Once Before Washing It?, page 127)
- Distilled white vinegar
- Laundry brush
- Washing machine cleaning tab

THIS IS HOW WE DO IT

Sort Your Shit Out, One Load at a Time

Let's not get complicated! I want to relieve you of your wash anxiety. If you want your darks to be dark, your colors to be bright, your whites

to be white, and your delicates to be not damaged, then sorting into those four basic categories will do the trick:

- Darks
- Colors
- Whites
- Delicates

We all know that if you put a red hoodie in with your white socks, the socks will come out pink. That's pretty intuitive. Sorting laundry is just thinking it through before it goes in the wash. Laundering your black jeans with a white T-shirt will have the T-shirt coming out gray. If you want to take it a step further, you can do separate loads for sheets, towels, and bedding. Your delicate blouse should not go in the same load with your sturdy towels. And so on and so forth.

10 EASY CHEAT SHEET LAUNDRY TIPS FROM THE LAUNDRY LESBIAN

- Stop using fabric softener. Replace it with distilled white vinegar or nothing at all. Softener buildup will ruin your clothes and machine.

- Stop using dryer sheets. Switch to balls or just dry your clothes for a shorter amount of time (it's the overdrying that causes static). Dryer sheets ruin your clothes and coat the sensors in your dryer that tell it when the clothes are dry.
- Use cold water for everything but whites. Hot water will fade colors and darks and it's much kinder to the environment.
- Check your pockets before you toss clothing in the machine.
- Clean your washing machine with a cleaning tab or good old elbow grease.
- Don't overuse detergent.
- After a wash, check to see if your stains came out before you toss them into the dryer. The dryer will set stains in. Re-treat stains until they're out, then dry.
- Undo the buttons on your shirts so the holes and threads don't get strained and stretched.
- Make sure the zippers are zipped. If they're undone, they can get caught on clothing and the drum itself, damaging both. They can also scratch the glass window.

BONUS TIP:
(Because 11 Tips Didn't Sound as Good)

- To avoid the case of the infamous missing sock mystery, wash all of the socks in a mesh bag and you'll never lose one again . . . even better, keep a bag in every basket so that they go right in the bag as soon as they come off.

What's the Frequency, Kenneth?

Like I said, I do laundry every day. Laundry can get away from you *fast*. Doing it every day is how I stay sane. Smaller families or single people might say they're waiting for the hamper to be full to do a wash. The key is to just keep doing it, so you don't end up unconscious underneath a mountain of laundry that has sneakily taken over your house and your life.

Another thing to consider in terms of your frequency is odor. Seventy percent of the dirt on your laundry—which isn't really dirt, it's skin, sweat, sebum, lotions, soaps—is invisible. So, you can actually go multiple wears before you need a wash if you're just going by looks. But the average adult sweats about 3 quarts per day (but it could be up to 10). I know, I know, you're off to google that fact, that's fine, I'll wait. The book and I will be here when you get back.

	CLOTHING		LINENS
After every wear	Socks Underwear Undershirts Exercise clothing T-shirts Face masks Swimsuits Tank tops Whites	*Daily*	Dish cloths
2-3 wears	Dress shirts Blouses Tights, leggings, yoga pants Bras Pants Dresses	*2-3 Days*	Hand towels Dish towels
4-5 wears	Jeans Suits Sleepwear Hoodies Sweaters	*Weekly*	Towels Bath mats Sheets

	CLOTHING		LINENS
When the mood strikes	Footwear Jackets/coats (1–2 times per season recommended) Neckties	*When the mood strikes*	Curtains Bathrobes Comforters and duvets (1–2 times per year recommended) Car seat covers Stroller covers Shower curtains Lunch bags Mattress covers Bed skirts

WANT TO WEAR SOMETHING MORE THAN ONCE BEFORE WASHING IT? MARK IT!

If you're like me, there are some things you wear more than once before tossing it in the machine, but it can be easy to forget just how many times you've worn it. A good ol' sniff test will do, but if you want to integrate a more structured system into your washing cycle, homemade or store-bought bookmarks (or anything you can hang over the neck of a hanger) will do. Make a bunch with different numbers on them, signifying how many times an item has been *worn*. If you're comfortable wearing a hoodie four times, and you took it off the hanger that had a "3" on it, you know to toss it in the wash instead of hanging it back up. Now you know how to keep track.

The Three D's

So, there you are, standing in front of the machine. At the risk of stating the obvious (and feel free to skip ahead if you're a pro), I'm going to outline the most important things to know about doing the wash. And if you're *not* a pro, have no shame. I recently came across a woman in her fifties, I'm not going to name names or anything, that would be unfair to my sister, who thought the detergent pods went into the same drawer as the liquid detergent, not realizing that you're supposed to throw those directly into the drum. I know someone else who thought you had to cut them open and squeeze the detergent out. Again, I don't want to name names, I wouldn't want to call her out twice. Maybe I just blew your mind because you thought those things, too. That's okay! Let me introduce you to the three D's: the drum, the drawer, and the dryer. The drum is where you put detergent pods, boosters, and scent beads. The drawer is for liquid/powder detergent, fabric softener, vinegar, and disinfectant. The dryer is for dryer balls and dryer sheets. Easy, now you know. Basically, no question is a stupid one, and you're never too old to learn.

Cold Water Is Almost Always Fine

The only time I do a hot wash is for a disinfect or white cycle: cloths, towels, sheets, whites, but all other times I use cold water. Cold water thoroughly cleans clothing and doesn't fade colors. Most detergents nowadays are actually formulated to work better in cold. Psychologically you may think they are getting cleaner in hot water. Bubbles, foam, scent, warmth—people think that all means clean. But it's more about how the ingredients work in the product we use that's important.

Liquid, Pods, Powder, or Strips—
How Do I Choose?

People always ask me what the best laundry detergent is and I will tell you, but first let's talk about what makes one detergent different from another. Are all detergents created equal? Absolutely not. It usually boils down to ingredients that are not always listed on the label, so you may need to look them up online. But ingredients will almost always affect price and how well your detergent performs. Ingredients like enzymes, surfactants, and brighteners will be reflected in the price because detergent formulas and the science behind them take years of research and development. Enzymes are the biggies, though. These have changed the way that we do laundry. They allow us to clean clothes in lower water temperatures while using less detergent, which is also better for the environment.

What most people are looking for in a detergent is stain-removal power, whitening, brightening, and scent. Just remember that whitening, brightening, and scent have absolutely nothing to do with cleaning.

So, 70 percent of soil on clothes comes from us. For example, sweat and body oil contain protein that regular soap can't remove. That's when the enzymes kick in: They're the stain removers. Different enzymes remove different stains and the greater number of different enzymes in your detergent, the more stain-removal power it will have. Just like enzymes break down food in the body, they break down stains in your laundry. Enzymes are naturally occurring and they're biodegradable.

As I've said before, premium detergents are premium for a reason. They do have some pretty cool ingredients. In contrast, lower price detergent can lack key ingredients, and some will wash your clothes about as well as plain water would. Detergent is something that everyone uses, so it's a very competitive market. Laundry detergent is available in four main forms: liquid, powder, pods, and strips.

I always use a quality liquid detergent, usually Persil or Tide.

Although that's what I prefer, have a look at the list below and what suits you best.

FORM	PROS	CONS
Liquid	Dissolves well in any water temperature Can be used to pretreat stains More cost effective per load than other methods	Packaging is not environmentally friendly Easy to overuse Recommended amounts are too much
Powder	Lowest cost per load by a significant amount Packaging is recyclable Has the longest shelf life	Doesn't dissolve as well in cold water Must be made into a paste to use it as a pretreater for stains Always needs to be kept completely dry to avoid clumping
Pods	Prevent overuse Convenient Long shelf life Ingredients are separated until pod dissolves	Can't be used for pretreating Poisoning hazard for children Need two for a large load but one may be too much for a small load Cost per load
Strips	Convenient Compact and lightweight and easy to store and transport Mess-free Prevent overuse Low-waste packaging Fewer chemicals, more natural ingredients, which means less scent and perfume	More expensive per load than traditional detergents Newest to the market, so hasn't yet been finessed Can't be used to pretreat stains Doesn't dissolve as well in cold water

A Little Detergent Goes a Long Way

The thing to remember is, no matter what detergent you are using, detergent companies are influencing how much you use. They give you these caps and scoops to easily measure out detergent for your load. The secret is, though, that you will rarely need more than 2 tablespoons to clean your clothes. I know it's hard to believe, but that is because we have been led to believe that more detergent equals more clean. They want you to use more, so you buy more. Clever, but it isn't getting past this laundry genius. Two tablespoons is the same amount as a small shot glass, so my little tip is, dust off that shot glass you got from your week in Mexico and move it to the laundry. (See, you did find a use for it after all.)

DETERGENT (MEDIUM LOAD)	TRADITIONAL WASHER	HIGH-EFFICIENCY WASHER
Liquid	2–4 tablespoons	2 tablespoons
Powder	2–4 tablespoons	2 tablespoons
Pods	1 pod	1 pod
Strips	1 strip	1 strip

Fragrance Doesn't Mean Clean

A nice scent can trick you into thinking that something is cleaner than it actually is. When you hire someone to come clean your house, it had better smell good at the end, right? Because otherwise, what did you pay for? But that's a psychological trick, and there is a reason for it. Scent is closely connected to memory and emotion, and this connection is what makes smell so different from our other senses. Surely you have smelled something and instantly been catapulted to a specific place or time from your past. As children, our brains begin forming connections between smells and events, people, or things associated with the scent. This is why you may smell an aftershave and immediately think of your grandfather, or the smell of coconuts may instantly remind you of that beach vacation from years ago. This connection of smells to individual memories is the reason not everyone enjoys the same smells. We often buy detergent and cleaning supplies that remind us of our childhood homes.

Chemical scent manufacturers are in the know. They use the connection between scent, memory, emotion, and association when introducing new scents. Many focus on scents that we the consumer associate with "clean." Scents like lemon, breeze, linen, fresh, floral are always top sellers. What even is the smell of fresh? Or breeze? Breeze from where? Trust me, unscented products work just as well as the perfumy ones.

Drop the Fabric Softener

Put down the fabric softener and walk away. I know I mentioned this already, but I'm going to repeat: I'm not a fan. Yes, they smell pretty, but that's about where the fun stops. They create a chemical barrier that sticks to fabric to make it feel soft, but it's not doing your laundry any favors. Over time, this barrier will just cause buildup on both your laundry and your machine. The barrier causes your towels to become less absorbent, your clothes will have almost a creamy feel to them. Because of the high number of chemicals in fabric softener, it can also cause skin irritation, so it's not recommended for people with sensitive skin.

Ask yourself why you're using fabric softener. Are you just using it because your mother did? Just because you think you have to? Because it smells nice? If you're just using fabric softener because of the scent, in my opinion, there are better options to add scent to your wash without the downsides that come with using fabric softener. (I'll tell you about those in just a minute.)

If you still want soft clothes, just add ¼ cup distilled white vinegar to the fabric softener dispenser in your washer or to a fabric softener ball. The vinegar will soften your laundry and—bonus!—keep your washing machine smelling fresh and clean.

ALTERNATIVE USES FOR LIQUID FABRIC SOFTENER

Now that you are immediately stopping your fabric softener use, you might have some left over. No need to waste it, there are other uses for your beloved fabric softener. Here are just a few:

- To remove wallpaper, mix equal parts softener and warm water in a spray bottle.
- To refresh your car, carpets, and furniture, mix 2 quarts water, 1 capful fabric softener, and 2 tablespoons baking soda.
- If there's a spot in your home where bugs/mice seem to gather, mix water and a capful of fabric softener in a spray bottle. Spray wherever they are: The strong smells should keep them away.
- Make slime for the kids.
- Get the funky garbage disposal odor out by adding ice and a tablespoon or two of fabric softener into the sink and let it run for several minutes.
- Rid your kid's favorite doll of knotty hair with a bit of softener!

But Embrace Scent Beads!

Boy, do I ever have a love affair with these little things. If you're looking for a way to add scent to your wash, scent beads are for you. Scent beads are tiny little beads of fragrance, not fabric softener, that you add directly to the drum of your washing machine. They may be tiny, but they pack quite a punch. They leave no nasty buildup, unlike our old friend fabric softener, and they are safe for all machines. I normally only use half of the recommended amount.

What Is the Difference Between Unscented and Fragrance-Free?

It can be confusing, but there is a big difference. If something is labeled unscented, it may contain chemicals that neutralize or mask the odor of ingredients in the product. If you are allergic to a certain fragrance, you may still have a reaction to something unscented because it's still present, the odor's just been masked. Fragrance-free means that no fragrance or masking chemicals are used in the product at all.

There's a New Bleach on the Block

Oxygenated bleach is a natural, safe, and gentle alternative to traditional chlorine bleach. It removes stains and brightens your whites without having to worry about burning your skin or ruining a piece of clothing. It is also a mild but effective disinfectant.

Oxygenated bleach can be used in any water temperature but is most effective in hot water temperatures. When added to water, it releases oxygen, which acts as a powerful stain and dirt lifter. Oxygenated bleach will brighten and whiten better than chlorine bleach and without the hazardous toxicity, environmental impact, or the yellowing. The best part is that it is color safe, so it won't bleach your colored clothing or fade the colors.

Prewashing New Gear Is Not Required but It Never Hurts

While we're getting all chemical-y . . . ever wondered why your new clothes smell a little funny, like chemicals or even mothballs? I hate to be the one to break it to you, but those are chemicals and ones you should know about. Let's talk about the mothball smell: That's naphthalene, which is what mothballs are made of. Maybe you're smelling pickles: That smell is formaldehyde (yes, the stuff used to embalm dead bodies). Naphthalene and formaldehyde are the most common, but fabrics and clothing are treated with all sorts of different chemicals, usually to stop mold, mildew, and bacteria from forming during transportation and storage. Chemicals are also applied for texture, color, wrinkle resistance, or even as an insecticide. Some of these chemicals can cause contact dermatitis, and manufacturers don't have to disclose what chemical treatments they've used. Let's not forget the other people who have tried on the clothes before you purchased them, which could put you at risk of getting other fun things like lice, scabies, ringworm, fungus, or even bedbugs. (I've really made you stop and think now, haven't I?) To avoid irritation, you should always wash your new clothes before you wear them. I know it feels great to put on a brand-new outfit, but for me, it's not worth the risk.

STUFF YOU PROBABLY DIDN'T KNOW YOU COULD CLEAN IN THE WASHING MACHINE

- Shoes (see If the Shoe Fits, page 138)
- Pillows (cotton, feather, down, fiberfill), but not foam
- Car mats
- Makeup sponges, kitchen sponges, and bath sponges, including loofahs
- Stuffed animals
- Shower curtains (see How to Wash a Shower Curtain, page 137)
- Reusable grocery bags
- Mouse pads
- Belts, but not leather ones
- Yoga mats
- Lunch bags
- Backpacks
- Curtains made of polyester or rayon
- Small plastic toys (in zippered mesh bags)
- Mop heads

- Hockey equipment (everything but the skates and sticks)
- Down jackets
- Electric blankets
- Weighted blankets

You Don't Ever Need to Hand-Wash, but If You Want to, Here's How

We hand-wash delicate materials because we don't want to beat them up, tossing them around willy-nilly and without care. But here's the thing: That's exactly what the gentle cycle is for. Always read the label, but chances are, if something says "hand wash," you can just translate that to "gentle cycle" on your washing machine with cold water and a gentle detergent.

If you're feeling fancy and you want to actually hand-wash something, follow these simple steps:

1. Add a small amount of gentle detergent to a sink filled with water (temperature according to the label).
2. Add item and gently move in water to loosen soil. Allow the item to soak for 15 to 20 minutes.
3. Rinse by running the item under cold water until the water runs clear (which means the detergent is gone).
4. Place the item on a towel and loosely roll up like a burrito to remove excess water.
5. If the item is small, you can put it in a salad spinner to remove the excess water.
6. Hang or lay flat to dry.

Consider a Mesh Bag for Delicates

Some lingerie, such as fancy bras and underwear, can be damaged in the wash because of their hooks and straps that can get tangled or caught on other items, possibly ruining those as well. The best practice for these is to use a mesh bag. Just put delicate items in a mesh bag (sometimes referred to as a lingerie bag) and wash them in the machine. Be sure not to overstuff the bag. Just like overstuffing your machine, the items won't get thoroughly clean if they don't have room to move around somewhat freely. Remember that you want the detergent and water to easily move through and around the items during a wash cycle. You can put several (two or three) bags in the same wash together, but since you are using the delicate cycle, wash your delicates separately from your other clothes. They will still come out just as clean, but the bag will prevent any damage, snagging, or tangling during the wash.

HOW TO WASH A SHOWER CURTAIN AND LINER IN THE MACHINE

Shower curtains and liners can get really grungy! They live in a hot and damp environment and are in constant contact with hard water, soap scum, and (let's face it) body scum. If you've gotten into the habit of just replacing your curtain and liner when it starts to look gross, save your money! Whether you have a plastic or fabric curtain and liner, you can wash them all the same way.

1. Remove the shower curtain and liner from the rod. Place them in the washing machine with two or three towels. (The towels will help scrub the curtain, especially if it's plastic.)
2. Add your laundry detergent as usual plus ½ cup baking soda directly to the drum (this adds even more scrubbing power).
3. Once they've been washed, remove the curtain and liner and simply hang them back up on the rod to air-dry before your next shower. Do not ever put a plastic curtain or liner

in the dryer—they'll melt. You *can* put fabric ones in the dryer, but you run the risk of shrinking them (and though I'm sure you have lovely ankles and feet, I'm guessing you don't want them on display while you wash your bod).

Take Extra Care with Specialized Activewear

Workout clothes with sweat-wicking technology (e.g., Dri-FIT) require extra steps so they don't stink. First, make sure they're completely dry before you throw them in a hamper. (If they're soaked in your sweat and just sit in a clump, even for a few hours, getting the stink out will be even harder.) Most activewear is made from synthetic fibers that have a natural attraction to oils. The oil promotes bacterial growth and bacteria is the cause of the smell. Once you're ready to launder them, first soak them in a sink full of cold water with 1 cup distilled white vinegar for about 30 minutes. Then turn them inside out (so the soap comes into contact with the dirtiest parts) and throw them in the machine with your usual detergent—plus 1/2 cup baking soda—on cold. Remember, never use fabric softener: Among its other faults, it will destroy the moisture-wicking technology of the activewear. For tough odors, specialty products are available, specifically to remove odor from athletic wear. Downy Rinse and Refresh is the most effective and my favorite.

If the Shoe Fits

If this is the first time you are hearing that you can wash your shoes in the washing machine, lucky you, because I found out the hard way. When I was pregnant with my first child, I didn't anticipate morning sickness to be quite like what I got. I pictured having slight nausea, just in the a.m. hours, but, no. I threw up every five seconds, from sunup to sundown. When I ate, when I didn't eat, when I stood up, when I sat down, it didn't matter. I threw up more times than I thought possible. And when I did throw up, I mostly threw up on myself, and this included my shoes. I ruined every pair of shoes I owned, or so I thought. Out of sheer frustration one day, I just threw them into my washing machine. What did I have to lose, yet another pair of shoes? When they came out sparkly and fresh, I was amazed. My shoes weren't ruined after all. Now you might not be throwing up on your shoes every five seconds (or maybe you're reading this and you're pregnant and this is ringing true), but shoes, in general get dirty. They walk all kinds of places and get all kinds of dirty. Good news is most athletic shoes or canvas shoes are durable and safe to be washed in the machine. Just use some Dawn on a brush first to loosen dirt and then pop them in the wash on gentle. Toss in an old towel to reduce noise.

How About Electric Blankets?

Can you wash electric blankets? The answer is absolutely, yes, you can. In fact, you should wash one before you use it for the first time, much like any other bedding. Many fabrics and materials are treated with chemicals in order to prevent mold and mildew and myriad other reasons during the manufacturing and shipping process. For this reason you should always wash bedding before you use it. First check the condition of the blanket to make sure it's in good shape. Make sure that there are no wires poking through . . . in which case you probably need a new blanket. Next, disconnect the power source. Make sure the blanket fits into your washing machine comfortably. If it is too big for your home machine, take it to the laundromat and use an industrial machine. Wash the blanket on a gentle/delicate cycle with cold water and gentle detergent. Because the gentle/delicate cycle is short, you're going to let the machine fill up first, pause the cycle, and let the blanket soak for 10 to 15 minutes. Then let it run through the rest of the cycle. Next you can put it in the dryer on low heat for 10 to 15 minutes and then let it air-dry for the remainder until it's completely dry.

How Do You Wash Weighted Blankets?

Weighted blankets have become a very popular item to own. It seems like in the last few years everyone has one and everyone who has one has the same question, how do I wash it? If you have a cover on your weighted blanket, that's great, because that's going to reduce the frequency with which you need to wash the actual blanket. Washing the blanket itself isn't tricky. The first thing you need to do is to figure out what's inside the blanket that gives it its weight (filler). Most weighted blankets that you buy online or in a store nowadays contain either glass microbeads, steel beads, or plastic pellets and are machine washable. If your blanket is weighted with sand, rice, other grains, or beans, you will want to avoid putting it in the washer or dryer. Next you will need to figure out how much your blanket weighs in order to determine where you're going to wash it. Most home washing machines and dryers have a weight capacity of 15 to 20 pounds, so if your blanket is more than 15 pounds, I would recommend that you take it to the laundromat and wash it in an industrial machine. Start by pretreating if you have any big stains, or any stains that you really want to concentrate on. Use a Dawn and baking soda paste and an old toothbrush on stains. Next wash it on a gentle/delicate cycle in cold water with gentle detergent. Do not use bleach or fabric softener. Next put it in the dryer using low heat. If you would rather skip the dryer, you can lay it flat to dry. Laying it flat is best to avoid the risk of the filler dropping to one end if hung over something to dry.

Pillow Talk

Most pillows filled with cotton, feather, down, and fiberfill can be washed in a washing machine. They can be washed on a gentle/delicate cycle in cold or warm water using your regular detergent. They can be air-dried or dried on low heat with tennis balls (the weight of the tennis balls helps to avoid clumping). Stopping the dryer to massage the pillows every 10 minutes will ensure that the filling remains evenly dispersed. Foam pillows are the exception. Foam pillows can never be washed in a washing machine or dried in a dryer due to melting and risk of fire. Foam pillows can be spot-cleaned by hand and air-dried only. Use a Dawn and baking soda paste for light staining. For blood or significant sweat stains, use some hydrogen peroxide to cover the stain. Allow it to sit for 15 to 30 minutes, then wipe with a clean cloth. Repeat if necessary until the stain is removed. Pillows should be washed every 3 to 6 months and replaced every 2 to 3 years.

DON'T FORGET ABOUT YOUR REUSABLE SHOPPING BAGS

Times have changed, and single-use plastic bags are becoming less and less common. You probably have a million reusable shopping bags. But those bags come into contact with so many germs, bacteria, and other yucky stuff, you have to wash them! Don't worry, washing them is easy. For plastic bags, you can clean them using a disinfectant wipe or soap and water and air-dry. For fabric bags, if there's a bottom insert, remove it before washing (even if the insert is covered in fabric, it is probably a piece of cardboard), then turn the bags inside out and wash them with regular detergent and air-dry.

Some Notes About Laundromats

Plenty of people do not have washer-dryers at home, including me when I moved house. I used a laundromat for a whole year. Laundromats are great because you can do six loads at once, which is much faster than being limited to one load at a time at home. All the guidance above (and below) applies to you with some modifications.

- Presort your laundry at home to save time. Use pillowcases, laundry bags, baskets, garbage bags, or a utility cart—whatever's easiest for you to transport to and from the laundromat.
- Pretreat your stains at home. That'll save time, too.
- Always bring extra garbage bags with you, that way if it's raining on the way home, you can avoid getting your freshly dried clothes wet by putting them in the bags.

- If they have a large-capacity machine, I know the temptation is strong to just put all of your clothes into one load. Sorting still applies. Saving a few dollars isn't worth ruining your clothes.
- Make sure the machines that you've picked are clean. Some may be coated in old detergent—meaning they weren't cleaned after last use—and you don't want someone else's residue, bleach, or who knows what else on your clothes. Check the compartments to make sure they're not dirty or gummy. If they are, find another machine. Look in the drum for culprits like ChapStick, pens, crayons, and any other little villains waiting to ruin your day or possibly your relationship when you have to explain to your partner why you have someone else's underwear in your wash. (Also, eww, strangers' underwear.)
- Bring antibacterial wipes for the folding tables. The last thing you want to do is lay down your fresh clothes into invisible mystery gunk.
- Fold your clothes straight out of the dryer. The temptation to just throw them in a bag and fold at home is strong, but let's be honest: You're not going to want to do that when you get home, either, so you're going to end up with wrinkles.
- Bring your own soap and supplies. Most laundromats don't offer a huge selection and sell expensive, questionable-quality

detergent. The single-use packs they peddle will also cost you more per load than if you bring your own.

- Now that we've decided it's best to bring your own detergent, lugging your own bottle or box to the laundromat isn't ideal. Instead, I would recommend premeasuring your liquid or powder ahead of time. Or perhaps think about alternatives. Pods and laundry detergent strips can be more convenient.
- Set a timer on your phone. If you want to run errands while your wash is doing its thing, just set a timer on your phone so you know when to come back for your laundry.
- Don't forget your coins—and this book for a little light reading while you wait.

DRYING

This Is Where You Master the Skill of Keeping Your Clothes the Same Size They Were Before Going into the Dryer

. . .

Let's get ready to tumble! We've all been there, when you've put your favorite sweater in the dryer only to realize an hour later that the only thing that sweater is fitting is your kid's doll. I know the dryer can feel like the giant hot monster sometimes. What can I put in there? Will this get ruined? How long should I dry this for? What are all those settings on my machine? Well, you've come to the right place. Let's dry the damn wash!

1O EASY CHEAT SHEET DRYER TIPS FROM THE LAUNDRY LESBIAN

- Shake out your clothes when you remove them from the washer before putting them in the dryer. It will help prevent wrinkles and tangling. This is especially true for sheets.
- Dry full loads of laundry when possible, rather than a single item or a few items at a time. They will dry faster and it's a more efficient use of energy.

- Don't overstuff the dryer. The clothes need room to tumble. The air needs to be able to circulate in and around the clothes to fully dry and reduce wrinkles.
- Choose the right setting for your clothes. Follow the instructions on the label.
- Don't open the door midcycle. Opening the door midcycle allows hot air to escape, which will increase the drying time.
- Don't overdry your clothes. Overdrying is the leading cause of static.
- Remove clothes from the dryer as soon as they are dry. The longer they sit in the machine, the more wrinkles you will have.
- Wash and dry bedsheets on their own. Sheets are infamous for twisting and trapping other items inside them. To avoid frustration, keep them separate.
- Use the dryer back-to-back. Drying loads of laundry one after the other will reduce energy costs, because the dryer won't have to warm up each time.
- Remove wrinkles with ice. If you just want to refresh or dewrinkle an item, you can toss a few ice cubes in the dryer. This will create steam and it's a quick fix if you don't want to get the iron out.

TOOLBOX

- Dryer balls
- Tennis balls

THIS IS HOW WE DO IT

How Hot Is Too Hot?

Use your wash settings as a guide. Anything that requires the gentle/delicate cycle in the washer needs similar care in the dryer, and that means low heat. Every item will be different. It's best to read and follow the instructions on the labels, especially if you're unsure.

Let's Talk About My Balls

If you know me, you know that I love my balls—dryer balls that is. Dryer balls come in plastic, rubber, and wool versions and they work by bouncing between wet layers of clothing. The separation of the clothing allows warm air to dry your clothes more quickly. They also reduce static while absorbing moisture, adding a bonus layer of drying to the process. You can also make DIY dryer balls: Roll up sheets of aluminum foil into tight balls, about the size of a tennis ball. They will help to reduce static. The aluminum foil balls can be reused for 1 to 2 months. It's the most cost-effective method for reducing static. I'm a big fan of wool dryer balls, and I use 3 to 6 balls per load.

But I'm sure you've heard of the age-old dryer sheet debate? Wait, maybe I started the debate. Should I use dryer sheets? Dryer sheets are something we have been programmed to believe we need. Yes, they control static; however, the static is controlled by chemicals. These chemicals not only stick to your clothes, but they also stick to the sensors in your dryer that let your dryer know when the clothes are dry. They will most definitely shorten the life span of your machine. Dryer sheets contain synthetic chemicals that coat the fabric and can cause allergic reactions. Sure, they provide a lovely scent, and if you really miss it, you can always add a few drops of essential oils to a wool dryer ball and that will disperse the scent while drying. Heck, they even sell scented dryer balls. Cutting out the dryer sheets also saves that time, and that time, and the other time you noticed a dryer sheet hanging out of the bottom of your pants in the line at the bank, at work, or at that party?

If it comes down to dryer sheets vs. dryer balls, for me, it's dryer balls for the win every time. They are also the most cost-effective and environmentally responsible choice.

Side note: While we're on the topic of balls, tennis balls also come in handy with drying certain items. Not to be confused with dryer balls, adding a few tennis balls in your dryer will help to fluff up certain filled or heavier items—like down coats, comforters, and pillows. Just make sure to use clean ones, not the ones you play fetch or mixed doubles with.

ALTERNATIVE USES FOR DRYER SHEETS

Now that I've crushed your dreams and told you to stop using dryer sheets, you're probably wondering, What am I supposed to do with the forty-seven boxes of dryer sheets I stocked up on? Fear not! They have alternate uses. You can use dryer sheets to:

- Dust computer screens and keyboards
- Dampen and then wipe on your windshield and bumper to remove dead bugs and dirt
- Dust your dashboard
- Repel mosquitoes: Pop one in your pocket
- Swipe over your hair to combat frizz
- Make stinky shoes or boots smell better: Stick one in each shoe
- Add a fresh scent to a drawer, garbage can, or suitcase
- Dust blinds
- Dust baseboards

Nice Rack

I have a great rack. My in-machine dryer rack is one of the sexiest things in my home. Yes, it's possible your machine came with a dryer rack, too. (No, I cannot help you find it if you have no idea where it is.) If your machine didn't come with a rack, you can likely buy one. A dryer rack is like a shelf that sits in your dryer on which you can place items you don't want to tumble. They're particularly great for shoes and other items that clunk around when they're being dried.

If your ears perked up when I mentioned drying shoes without the clunk but you don't want to go to the expense of getting a dryer rack, you can still jerry-rig your own anticlunk operation. Tie a knot

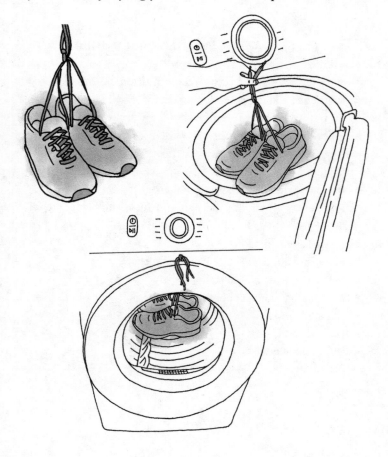

at the end of your laces to connect the shoes together. Then, shut your laces into the end of the door of the dryer so the knot is on the outside and the shoes are inside. This hack will prevent your shoes from tumbling. Always use a low heat setting since drying your shoes on high heat can loosen the glue holding the shoes together. If airdrying, avoid placing them in direct sunlight as this can cause fading.

Lay Flat If the Tag Says to Lay Flat

If the tag says to dry your sweater flat, there's good reason. The weight of the wet fabric can cause it to stretch if it's on a drying rack (the same way you can end up with bunny ears if you dry something on a hanger). Instead, remove as much water as you can from your item by laying a dry towel down on a flat surface and placing the item on the towel. Then roll (like a burrito)—gently, don't squeeze—just enough to absorb the extra water. (If you're comfortable, you can also throw your garment in the dryer on a cool setting for a few minutes before you lay it flat.) Grab another dry towel and lay the item flat, flipping it over once one side is dry. Use any flat surface you can find, e.g., the top of your washer, dryer, or a table. If you have a drying rack, make sure that the item is laid on the top of the rack, as though it were a table, not through the slats.

STAIN REMOVAL

This Is Where You
Get the Damn Stains Out

. . .

I'M A MOTHER OF THREE, SO I KNOW STAINS HAPPEN. THEY happen to the best of us. I find that on the days I decide to wear a white shirt, gravity malfunctions and more coffee ends up on my top than in my mouth.

Ninety percent of the time, a quality detergent used as a stain remover to pretreat a stain will remove it; however, if not, I prefer making my own stain remover. I know what's in it, it's cheaper as I already have the products in my house, and I know it's effective. If you'd like to give it a go, check out the list below.

If you're the kind of person who wants to just buy a stain remover from the store to treat your stains, there's nothing wrong with that. They're convenient and most will do the job. Just buy whatever you like and follow the instructions exactly. If a stain remover says to leave it on for 5 minutes, leave it on 5 minutes.

TOOLBOX

- Dish soap
- Laundry detergent
- Hydrogen peroxide (see Rule of Thumb, on page 151)
- Baking soda
- Cotton balls
- Distilled white vinegar

- Rubbing alcohol
- Toothbrush
- Acetone nail polish remover
- Dry-erase marker
- Brushes varying in stiffness
- Cloths
- Shaving cream or dry shampoo

Rule of thumb: When you're making homemade stain remover, if the particular kind you're making (like some I suggest below) has hydrogen peroxide as an ingredient, you cannot make it ahead of time. Stain remover with hydrogen peroxide must be made in smaller quantities as needed because it is water with an extra oxygen molecule attached (H_2O_2 instead of H_2O). The extra oxygen is relatively loosely bound, making it a highly reactive chemical eager to oxidize any other molecules around it. It can break down into plain water when it's exposed to light or mixed with other ingredients over a period of time. That's why peroxide bottles are dark brown! Hydrogen peroxide is an oxygen bleach and typically safe on colors (I know you don't want to believe this, but it's true). Congrats, you are now a science genius!

Rule of other thumb: Almost anything that doesn't contain peroxide *can* be made ahead of time and stored in a spray bottle or container, ready to use when you need it.

THIS IS HOW WE DO IT

Time Is of the Essence

When dealing with heavily stained or soiled laundry, it is best to attend to it immediately. Fast action is the key, because new stains are easier to remove than stains that have had time to set in.

To pretreat stains, apply a small amount of quality liquid detergent directly to the stain, rub, blot, or brush and let it soak in for 10 to 15 minutes. If you use powder, you can use a little water to make a paste. Wash as normal. Unfortunately, this process doesn't work if you only have laundry pods or strips. There will be stains that you can't imagine coming out, but a pretreat will give it the best chance. This may be all you need.

If you didn't get to it in time or the stain didn't come out, don't worry, there is still hope. Keep reading. Whatever you do, don't put it in the dryer. It will set the stain.

Common Stains and How to Make Them Scram

Recipe No. 1: Sweat (yellow armpits and ring around the collar), oil, coffee, lipstick, chocolate, deodorant, grass, berries

Ingredients

- 1 tablespoon Dawn dish soap
- 1 tablespoon hydrogen peroxide
- 1–2 tablespoons baking soda

Instructions

1. Mix together to make a paste.
2. If you have bigger and/or multiple stains, double (or triple, etc.) the recipe amounts.
3. Let the paste sit for 15 minutes, then scrub with an old toothbrush or cloth and wash as normal.

Recipe No. 2: Ink/marker

Ingredients

- Rubbing alcohol
- OR nail polish remover

Instructions

1. Try one and if it doesn't work, try the other.
2. Whichever you choose, put the solution on a cotton ball and dab the stain. Just make sure if it's an article of cloth-

ing that you have a cloth or a towel underneath the layer you are treating to protect the bottom layer from transfer. You may need to change the cloth several times throughout this process. Let it sit for 15 minutes and wash as normal.

Recipe No. 3: Blood

Ingredients

- Hydrogen peroxide

Instructions

1. Rinse under water (warm or hot water will set bloodstains).
2. Apply hydrogen peroxide, enough to cover the stain.
3. Let it sit for 15 minutes and wash as normal.

Recipe No. 4: Wet paint

Ingredients

- 1 tablespoon Dawn dish soap

Instructions

1. Dab wet paint with a cloth to remove as much as possible.
2. Apply the dish soap to the stain and let it sit for 15 minutes, then scrub with an old toothbrush or cloth and wash as normal.

Recipe No. 5: Dry paint

Ingredients

- Rubbing alcohol

Instructions

1. Scrape off as much of the dried paint as possible.
2. Apply the rubbing alcohol to a cotton ball or cloth and dab the stain. Just make sure if it's an article of clothing,

that you have a cloth or a towel underneath the layer you are treating to protect the bottom layer from transfer. You may need to change the cloth several times throughout this process. Let it sit for 15 minutes and wash as normal.

Recipe No. 6: Salt stains, soy sauce, wine

Ingredients

- Distilled white vinegar

Instructions

1. Cover the stain in vinegar and let sit for 15 minutes.
2. Scrub it with an old toothbrush, then wash as normal.

Recipe No. 7: Urine

Ingredients

- Distilled white vinegar
- Quality laundry detergent

Instructions

1. Cover the stain in vinegar and let sit for 15 minutes.
2. For larger stains or articles saturated in urine, soak the item in a sink or a bucket, with enough water to cover the article. Add 2 cups of vinegar and a cup of quality detergent. Let it sit for up to 30 minutes.
3. Wash as normal.

Recipe No. 8: Mustard, curry, turmeric

Ingredients

- Oxygenated bleach

Instructions

1. Soak in a bucket or sink with oxygenated bleach and water (hot is best) for 30 minutes to an hour.
2. The stains will turn dark red; don't panic, wash as normal.

Recipe No. 9: Sticker residue, mascara

Ingredients

- Rubbing alcohol
- Cloth or cotton ball

Instructions

1. Saturate the cloth or cotton ball with alcohol and cover the sticker residue completely. Let sit for 10 minutes. It should just peel off.
2. If it doesn't, don't scrub, just add a little bit more rubbing alcohol. You may need to pick at it slightly, but that's it. Then wash as normal.

QUICK TIPS FOR STAIN REMOVAL

- Check that stains have been removed before moving items to the dryer (see next tip). Drying a stain before it's removed will set the stain in, and it will be very difficult to remove it.
- Use a dry-erase marker to write on the washing machine, to remind yourself and others to check any stained item before it goes in the dryer to see if the stain has been removed. It will wipe right off.
- Be careful not to spread the stain while treating it. Keep the stain area confined so it doesn't transfer to the rest of the item.
- Use cotton balls for gentle dabbing (delicate materials) and a toothbrush for a more vigorous scrub (hardier stuff).
- Detergent stains (white streaks or marks) are the result of using too much detergent or overloading the machine with clothes. To reverse the stains, you must keep washing with no detergent until removed.
- For stains in a pinch or on the go, don't bother with club soda, it doesn't work any better than regular old water. Shaving cream or dry shampoo are pretty handy. Apply a little shaving cream or spray dry shampoo onto the stain. Dab excess with a cloth. It works because it's soap. Then wash as normal when you can.

STRIPPING

This Is Where You Take It All Off

. . .

WHILE POSSIBLY NOT AS SEXY AS THE KIND OF STRIPPING you may be envisioning, for me, it is at least as exciting (and definitely more rewarding).

Stripping is exactly what it sounds like, a super-deep-cleaning process that removes body oils, detergent residue, and built-up chemicals (from things like fabric softener and dryer sheets) from your laundry. Think of it like detailing your car instead of just taking it for a regular wash. Nothing fancy required here—you can DIY your own stripping solution and get those clothes squeaky clean.

You'll know when you need to strip if a particular item no longer looks, works, or feels the way it should. Your towels somehow no longer get you dry or things just look and feel kind of yucky.

But here's the thing, maybe you're shy. You don't ever have to strip if you don't want to! Maybe once your towels stop absorbing water, you'd rather just replace them. That's fine! If you'd rather replace your sheets when they're looking a little worse for the wear, okay. But if you don't want to spend the money on new things, stripping is a great alternative to getting your items back to their former glory.

Personally? I get a little charge from stripping something, it's like a little laundry-gasm.

Stripping is not a full-time gig. It's an aggressive form of cleaning and doesn't need to be done often. It's truly easy and totally worth it. And if you're ready to try it, let's go, it's time to strip.

TOOLBOX

- Borax
- Washing soda (sodium carbonate)
- Laundry detergent

THIS IS HOW WE DO IT

1. Combine ¼ cup Borax, ¼ cup washing soda, and ½ cup laundry detergent in a full sink, bucket, or tub of water. This can be done in a top-load washing machine if you are able to pause the cycle.
2. Place the items in the mixture and soak for 2 to 4 hours, stirring and moving the items around in the mixture about once every hour. The water will turn light brown to increasingly darker brown as the process works.
3. After the stripping process, wash as normal.

You Don't Have to Strip Everything— Just Anything with Buildup

Betty White, my daughter's beloved stuffy, is the filthiest thing ever. To my daughter, Betty White is perfect; to me she's a stinky, grimy, and foul little bunny. I thought I was a genius and sourced a fresh replacement Betty (which believe me, wasn't easy or cheap), but of course she only wants dirty old Betty. So when she gets intolerably filthy, while my daughter is asleep at night, I take Betty, I strip her, and before long, she's as good as new.

I mostly strip sheets, towels, clothes, and well-loved stuffed toys like Betty—anything that easily accumulates buildup. Buildup is anything you can see or feel: a halo of yellow from sweat, ghost stains from drool. Maybe you lather yourself in body butter. Maybe you coat your heels in Vaseline. Sometimes it's visual, sometimes it's something you can feel. If you think you have buildup, you probably do.

As much as I love to strip, I only do it occasionally. Stripping too often can be harsh on fabrics, so for me, it's an infrequent task. You can make the judgment on your own about when you need to strip, it all depends on who you sleep next to, how you launder, etc.

BLUING

This Is Where You Go Old-School

. . .

TOOLBOX

- Bluing liquid (Mrs. Stewart's is my favorite)
- Glass container

THIS IS HOW WE DO IT

Contrary to what it sounds like (and for maximum confusion), bluing is the process of making your fabrics appear whiter. In fact, it's a very effective way to get the whitest whites you've ever seen. Most people think bleaching makes your whites whiter but in fact over time bleaching (with chlorine bleach) regularly can yellow fabrics. Adding a blue pigment adds brightness to white fabrics, which counteracts the yellowing that occurs during regular laundering. The color blue tricks the eye into seeing the fabric as whiter.

Fabrics can get dingy for a lot of different reasons, including: color transfer from other fabrics; detergent and fabric softener residue; nicotine or air pollution; body oils and sweat; chlorine bleach; and lotions, potions, and deodorant.

Bluing has been around for over one hundred years. My grandmother used it, my mother used it, and who am I to break the tradition. In recent years, plenty of products have come on the market containing optical whiteners and brighteners, and bluing sort of fell by the wayside. These new products contain many chemicals, but bluing is a nontoxic, nonhazardous, and biodegradable way of achieving the same result. It's a time-tested method.

Bluing is easy: You simply follow the directions on the specific brand. The directions will vary depending on if you are using a front-loader or a top-loader or doing it by hand. The standard is that it is diluted in a glass container, as it can stain plastic, and it is either placed in the final rinse or soaked in the solution when doing it by hand.

IRONING

This Is Where It
Gets All Hot and Steamy

. . .

As a child, I spent many hours digging in and rummaging through all of my grandmother's closets, trunks, and boxes. She had some of the best treasures. Her stuff was better than any of my toys. My favorite treasure spot was her sewing room. She had an old round cookie tin filled with buttons that I would sort, count, and group, and I loved them. I spent hours sorting through those buttons.

Another of the boxes in that room had some sewing supplies and patches, but at the bottom of the box was a bag filled with iron-on appliqués. They were mostly flowers and birds and other (I now realize very UGLY) pictures and patterns. I asked my nan to show me how they worked and of course she did. She put a tiny bird on the pocket of my pants, and I was thrilled. She told me that I could take home all the iron-ons if I wanted them and I, of course, immediately put them in my "Nan bag" to take home.

Once I got home, I flew through the door ready to start my appliqué projects. I immediately thought what a great idea it would be to "fancy up" some of our boring plain pillowcases. The idea was gold, and I knew it. Soon everyone would know it. I headed straight for the linen closet and grabbed every pillowcase I could reach. With pillowcases and appliqués in hand, I went into the basement to set up my work station. After all, a professional appliquer needs a proper work station. Those pillowcases would be the most fantastic pillowcases anyone had ever seen. I decided it would be best to iron on the floor, so I set up and I was off. Flowers and birds were adorning the previously plain and boring pillowcases. I was so proud of the work I had started that I took the first few up to show my parents. I can still remember the look on my mother's face, which was a little angry, but her words were still sweet and encouraging. She pointed out how nice it would be to have these rubbing on her face as she slept (at age five I didn't hear the sarcasm). She even thought of something that I had not even considered: If your face ever got itchy during the night, there would be a built-in face scratcher at the ready.

Before I could even show all of my work, my father (a firefighter) asked what the smell was coming from the basement. It clicked. Both of my parents simultaneously yelled, "The iron!!" And ran downstairs to realize that I had been ironing on the floor and left the iron face down on the carpet while still on. After my father picked up the iron, we all stood and stared at the burn in my mother's '70s golden sunset shag carpet. They told me I was not to use the iron again without an adult present.

And I did just that! The next morning, I shoved that iron into my backpack with the rest of the appliqués and some pillowcases and headed off to kindergarten. My intention was to show the kids how to iron on the amazing appliqués. I wanted to share my knowledge and expertise with them. I assumed the teacher would be thrilled and of course she was an adult, so. . . . Well, as soon as I pulled it out, I barely got it plugged in when the teacher snatched the iron from me and called my parents. They were not happy and undoubtedly a little embarrassed based on the conversation I overheard them having with the teacher. It was the last time I was able to teach anyone how to iron . . . until now.

First things first: You don't ever have to iron if you don't want to. Ironing serves no purpose at all other than improving the appearance of your clothes (like my iron-on appliqués obviously did), so if you'd rather poke your eyes out than iron, skip it. You can live your whole life without ever owning or operating an iron. Ask my sisters, and yes, we have the same parents, I can't believe it either. It's all preference. Maybe you don't care what your collar looks like or if your pants have wrinkles. That's totally up to you. I can't stand to wear a button-up if it's not ironed, but that's me. So, if you're like me and you do like a crisp and wrinkle-free wardrobe, join me.

Side note? There are easy alternatives to ironing if you *do* like the look of a crisp piece of clothing, but not enough to actually iron it. Hang up your clothes in the bathroom while you're taking a hot shower, buy a steamer, or there are even wrinkle release sprays available that work great. The world is your wrinkle-free oyster.

Same discretion goes for *what* you iron. I iron my pillowcases, which may sound extreme to you, but allow me to introduce my mom, who ironed our *underwear*. Same rules apply: If the wrinkles bug you, consider ironing it, whether "it" is your table napkins or the sheets or even your socks (my mom ironed those, too).

TOOLBOX

- An iron or a steamer
- An ironing board (not necessary if you're using a steamer)

That's it! The iron is really the only compulsory tool for ironing—it's extremely hard to iron without one (go figure!)—along with its accompanying board. (A steamer is really just an iron alternative.) There are some optional add-ons if you're so inclined:

- Spray starch: an age-old staple that makes ironing go faster and smoother. Clothing has crisper collars and pleats that will look freshly ironed for much longer. Generally, spray starches are made with cornstarch. The "stiffness" will depend on the percentage of cornstarch in the specific product. Double starch will have a higher percentage.
- Ironing spray: pretty much just fancy water in a spray bottle. It will often have a fragrance and allows for smooth pressing with less drag on your iron. Moisture relaxes fibers and protects them from scorching. It will prevent sticking and scrunching during ironing as it will allow your iron to glide easily over your fabric. It lacks the stiffening element of starch. Water in a spray bottle is exactly the same as the ironing spray, but without the scent.
- Pressing cloth: a fancy way to say "an old piece of fabric" used to separate whatever you're ironing from the iron itself. These

are particularly good for delicate fabrics, like polyester and wool (where you want to make sure to avoid scorch marks). Think of a grilled cheese sandwich, with delicate fabrics as the cheese and the pressing cloth as the bread. If you put the iron directly on the cheese, you'd have a mess (and a waste of a perfectly good sandwich). You need the pressing cloth (or bread) as a buffer.

How to Choose the
Right Iron or Steamer

THIS IS HOW WE DO IT

TYPE OF IRON	DESCRIPTION	
Basic dry iron	A basic iron or a dry iron is just that! Very basic but gets the job done. It has few features. It generally consists of a metal soleplate and a very basic plastic housing.	
Steam iron	A definite step up from the basic dry iron, and the most popular and widely available. A steam iron has a small reservoir that holds water for the steam.	
Steamers (alternative to iron)	Steamers are handy when a shirt, dress, or jacket just needs a little steam to get wrinkles out. With a steamer, you can direct the steam at the wrinkled area without making contact with the fabric, so there's less work involved. There is no pressing required and the steaming is done with the item hanging up.	
Multidirectional iron	This is the Cadillac of irons. The five-star, all-inclusive, swim-up bar of irons, with more options than you could ever need but every option you really want. The best part is that they make the job faster! A multidirectional iron does not have a pointy end and a flat end. It has two points so that you can iron in all directions and in tight spots. Because of the double point, you can smooth out wrinkles more easily without having to turn and flip the iron or your body to get every part of the item or around buttons and zippers.	

Temperature Matters

A cold iron is useless. An iron that's too hot can damage your fabrics. Think about your curling iron, hair straightener, or even your oven: You want that baby ready to rock at the exact temperature you need it when you use it—that's why you preheat—but not so hot that it will immediately singe your hair or burn your lasagna. You have to do the same with an iron.

Distilled Water Is Best

If you are putting water into the reservoir of your iron, use distilled water. Distilled water lacks minerals and therefore won't clog your machine.

PROS	CONS
The most economical option but still gets the wrinkles out	No automatic shutoff option; no fancy fabric/temperature settings, no steam
Often comes with features like a retractable cord and automatic shutoff. They're also generally user-friendly and easy to store.	More expensive than a basic dry iron but still not so exorbitant that you'll have to remortgage your house.
They are super great for curtains, dresses, jackets, or items that are difficult to iron on a board.	They don't generally release continuous steam, so you have to manually activate the steam as needed. Some are on wheels, others handheld, so they range wildly in price and quality. You should always use distilled water (not convenient in a hotel).
They generally have easy seamless temperature adjustment, advanced steam features, bigger and easier to fill reservoirs, lighter weight, automatic shutoff, a retractable cord or even cordless with a docking station. These irons usually come with a better soleplate (less likely to stick to fabric) and more steam holes to make the job even easier.	This is the most costly option but well worth it for those who iron more than once a year.

Always Iron Delicates Inside Out

That includes silk, satin, rayon, linen, or anything else that you look at and think, "I should probably be careful with that."

Temperature Settings for Your Fabric

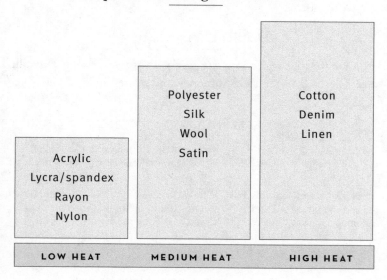

	Polyester	Cotton
Acrylic	Silk	Denim
Lycra/spandex	Wool	Linen
Rayon	Satin	
Nylon		
LOW HEAT	**MEDIUM HEAT**	**HIGH HEAT**

How to Iron Shirts and Pants

These are the most common items that need ironing. Once you know how to do these, you can apply the rules to almost anything else. When you are finished ironing, allow the iron to cool down for about 15 minutes before putting it away.

Shirts

1. Lay the shirt on the widest part of the ironing board, with the back of the shirt facing up with the arms draping over each side of the board.

2. Place the iron on the collar at the center and iron from
    the center out. Once you've removed the wrinkles from the
    collar, fold the collar back into it's "wearing position" and
    iron from the center working your way out.

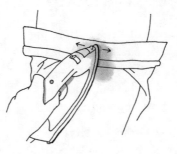

3. Iron the back of the shirt. Start with the back of the
    shoulder area and work your way down. You may need to
    reposition the shirt to ensure all areas have been ironed.

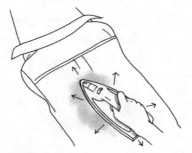

4. Now for the sleeves. Place one arm of the shirt on the
    ironing board so that it sits where you want the arm
    crease to be. Start ironing at the top where the seam is,

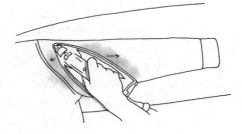

working your way down to the cuff, making sure there are no wrinkles between the layers so you aren't ironing in more wrinkles. Turn the sleeve and iron the opposite side and repeat the process with the other sleeve.

5. Now for the cuffs. Unbutton the cuff and lay flat. Start by ironing the inside of the cuff first and then turn over and repeat, making sure to go around the buttons, not over top.

6. Ironing the front of the shirt starts with the side with the buttons. Iron your way from the shoulder down, moving the iron around each button. Repeat on the other side.

Pants

1. If your pants have pockets, turn them inside out and start by ironing the pockets to prevent ironing in more wrinkles. Pull the pockets inside out and press them flat with the iron.

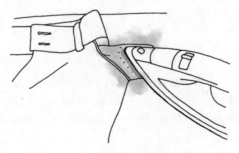

2. Lay one pant leg lengthwise on the ironing board, making sure the seams line up. Start ironing by moving the iron back and forth over the leg, starting at the top and moving toward the cuff. Turn the leg over and repeat on the other side. Repeat this process on the other leg.

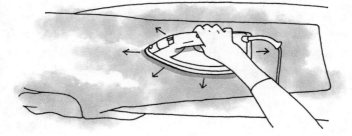

3. If you are looking for a crease in your pants, simply lay the pant leg on the ironing board so that the inseams are lined up and together. This will create a straight crease from the pockets on the top to the bottom and the same on the back.

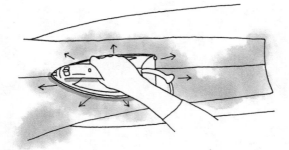

A NOTE ON STEAM CLOSETS

Welcome to the future, y'all, where there exists a Jetsons-like freestanding beautiful appliance called a steam closet. It is what it sounds like: a gleaming piece of machinery (picture a really skinny fridge) that simply slides against the wall, no plumbing required. Unlike a traditional steamer, a steam closet is a standalone closet in which you can place any item—a dress, pillows—and hit a button to sanitize by killing odor, bacteria, and allergens while removing wrinkles. It functions with two water reservoirs—one clean, one dirty (which you simply dump out). They'll cost you a pretty penny and they are not for everybody, but if you iron a lot and hate it, and you like pretty appliances, you could consider one.

THE ART OF PUTTING EVERYTHING AWAY

This Is Where You Realize Same-Day Service Is Better Than 3 to 5 Business Days

. . .

THIS IS THE PART OF LAUNDRY MOST PEOPLE DREAD, PUTTING everything away, probably because it's the part that takes the longest. And if you fall into that camp, I want you to remember this one thing before we start this chapter. You bought my book, the very lady who became famous on TikTok for this very thing. So, if it wasn't for folding and putting things away, our paths would never have crossed. Now, I can't promise you that this chapter is going to be as enjoyable as watching me fold on TikTok, without the smooth tones of my perfectly picked Motown classics (this is a book after all), but I can promise that when you master the art of putting things away, it will come with the most amazing feeling of satisfaction and accomplishment. So, in the words of Marvin Gaye (doing my best to get some Motown in here), let's get it on.

TOOLBOX

Putting things away doesn't *require* any tools—these are purely optional. Unlike, say, detergent when you're doing laundry, they're not crucial, so take what you want and leave what you don't. And if anything on this list makes you scratch your head—e.g., What the hell do zip ties have to do with hanging and folding? When did this turn into an episode of *CSI*?—just wait, my friend.

- Hangers, all different types (more on that below)
- Shower-curtain rings
- Soda-can tabs
- Zip ties
- Pipe cleaners
- Rubber bands

THIS IS HOW WE DO IT

Maximize Your Closet Space with DIY Inexpensive Hacks

Accessorizing your hangers can instantly grow them in width, depth, or length:

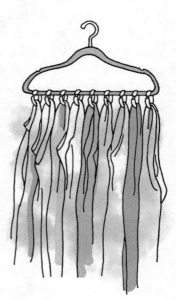

- Go wide: Put an entire pack of shower-curtain rings on the pant bar of one hanger and use them to hold lightweight items that are difficult to store. You can push scarves and ties through the rings or you can open the rings and clip belts, tank tops, and baseball hats. This is a great storage solution that doesn't add bulk to your closet.
- Go long: Looping a soda-can tab over the metal neck of a hanger adds a second place to hang *another* hanger. If your hanger neck is too wide for a

soda-can tab, you can make a zip tie into a loop and use that instead. This is another great storage solution that doesn't add bulk to your closet.

Rotate the Stuff in Your Drawers So It Doesn't Get Funky

Clothes in drawers over time can smell due to a lack of circulation and wear, so I don't always take the first pair of underwear. I will admit that I have forty-seven pairs of the exact same undies folded the exact same way. (I am well aware that this makes me weird and excessive but I am the Laundry Lesbian, what did you expect?) If I only kept taking out the first few, those other ones would just sit there. They need to be rotated so they don't live in there forever. Give 'em some air! Have you ever pulled things out that have been in the drawer forever? They smell. You don't know what they smell like, but they smell. This is when the drawer liners we talked about earlier come in handy.

Determine Which Hangers Are Best Based on Your Space (Not Just What You Think Looks Pretty)

Not all hangers are created equal, and one kind isn't intrinsically better than another—it all depends on your needs. You can even have a mix of hangers in your closet, though lots of people like the aesthetics of a matching set. Some people wouldn't be caught dead using the dry cleaner hangers, and other people use them exclusively. (In my house, we use them for roasting marshmallows. That's a free hack.)

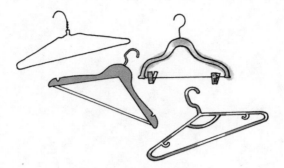

Plastic Hangers

When you put them side by side, they actually take up a lot of space just from the girth of the hanger (contrary to popular belief, girth isn't always a good thing). They bend easily (which is great), but also break easily (which is not great). They can also be slippery, but you can add traction with something as simple as a pipe cleaner or rubber band: Just wrap it around the end of the hanger, and suddenly your silk top isn't slipping, and you don't have to crisscross it over the hook.

Velvet and/or Felt Hangers

These are thinner and take up a lot less room from left to right. They're great for holding slippery little suckers like silk and satin in place. The downsides to these hangers is that it can be difficult to slide some fabrics over them, like cotton, running the risk of stretching things out, also, because they are thin, they do have a tendency to break easily.

Wood Hangers

Similar to plastic hangers, when you put them side by side they actually take up a lot of space just from the girth of the hanger (girth and wood . . . who knew this could ever be a bad thing). They look nice and some are durable. But often their pant bar is held on with a small tack or nail, and those give way after a while. They can be slippery but often they come with those notches that can be useful for items with thin straps.

Wire/Dry Cleaner Hangers

They're weak and thin, so if they're holding anything heavier than a dress shirt, they'll bend and put the bunny ears in your shoulders. But they're also cheap or free and so slim that they're good for anyone without lots of closet space.

Try Color-Coding!

People think I am a little extra for color-coding my closet and drawers, but I promise you it's for good reason and it's not just because it looks great. It's by far the easiest way to find an item. If you're looking for that one red T-shirt, instead of fingering your way through all the hangers (hold up, quick recap of the last few pages: 1: wood, 2: girth, 3: fingering ... carry on) or riffling through your drawers of neatly folded T-shirts—color coding will narrow it down to just a few items to look through. Unless of course you only wear red, then I guess you're color coding already.

Rolling with It

There's a reason the military teaches cadets to roll their gear. Rolling an article of clothing is called a ranger roll and the main concept is to create a pocket at one end and then roll it into itself. A ranger roll is compact and thus saves space, something that is especially useful when packing for a trip. The compact roll saves space in your suitcase, but also reduces wrinkles, and here's why: When clothing is folded and stacked in a suitcase, it moves around and items rub against each other and the suitcase, the result being an overstuffed bag and loads of wrinkles. When you're packing (or even if you have very limited drawer or cubby space at home), try rolling your clothes.

HOW TO PUT ON A DUVET COVER BY YOURSELF WITHOUT GETTING TRAPPED INSIDE IT

1. Turn the duvet cover inside out.
2. Place your hands inside the duvet cover, find and hold the two bottom corners. The ones on the nonbutton or zip end of the cover.
3. With your hands still holding the corners, find and hold the two corners of the duvet itself and hold one in each hand.
4. Flip the entire duvet cover over the duvet and give it a good shake, while still holding the corners.
5. Ensure the bottom corners are in place as well.
6. Now button the buttons or zip the zipper and smooth over the bed to complete.

Be Thoughtful and Goal-Oriented When You Think About How to Put Stuff Away

If you are failing to plan, you are planning to fail (something I say at every work conference if I've zoned out and I'm put on the spot to say what I've gotten out of the day). It can be applied to anything. Here for example. Remember that the goal is to make your life easier. When I'm folding my black tees, I fold them so that the pattern is showing. That way, I can tell them apart without unfolding them. On the other hand, I don't need to worry about that with my blue tee because I only have one. In every house I've lived in, I've done my clothes differently. Right now, my son hangs his pants folded over the hanger, but my daughter likes hers hung by the belt loops. For hoodies, I have hooks and I just hang them on hooks by the hood, layered on top of each other because I have so many. When I travel, I do a hoodie fold, where I fold it into the hood, so it fits more compactly.

Super-Easy Ways to Fold and/or
Hang Very Tricky Things

Fitted Sheets

1. Lay the sheet on a flat surface with the elastic facing up.
2. Turn the bottom corners inside out and put your hands into those corners.

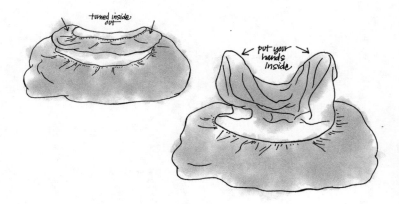

3. Slide your hands into the upper corners of the sheet.

4. Now you have a rectangle. Smooth out the sheet and fold
    it into thirds.

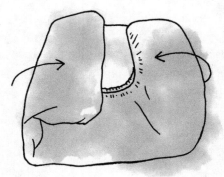

5. Fold into thirds again.

6. You did it! You actually folded a fitted sheet.

What a Drag!—Keeping Longer Items Up Off the Floor

This works for long dresses and long coats.

1. Lay the item face-up on a flat surface.
2. Fold one side into the middle. Do the same on the other side.
3. Place the hanger about a third of the way up the item.
4. Fold the bottom third of the item over the hanger bar.
5. Lift the hanger up and drape the straps or sleeves of the item over the hanger to complete.

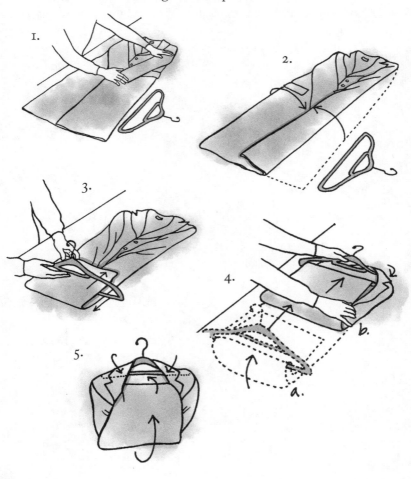

Folding Sweaters for a Hanger

1. Lay the sweater down on a flat surface, arms outstretched. Smooth to flatten.
2. Fold the sweater completely in half vertically, so both arms are on top of each other, like they're hugging.
3. Place the hanger upside down and diagonal on top of the sweater, so that the neck of the hanger is positioned just below the armpit.
4. Fold the body of the sweater over one side of the hanger.
5. Fold the arms of the sweater over the other side of the hanger.
6. Pull up by the hook and it's ready to hang. This way the sweater won't have any marks in the shoulders and is ready to wear.

Folding Irregularly Shaped Objects

If you've got an oddly shaped blanket or a one-shoulder dress, just make it a rectangle! If you can get whatever you're folding into a rectangle, you're golden. Once you do that, all folding is the same.

You may be thinking, Why would I *ever* need to fold a hooded towel, a round tablecloth, or an apron. What if you have no space in your closet or want to change over your closet seasonally? Get that sucker into a rectangle and then fold it like you would any other rectangle.

REPAIRING

This Is Where You Fix the Items You Were Just About to Throw Out

. . .

A s much as my kids are mortified by my TikTok, who's the first person they come to when their hoodie string has somehow come out? Yours truly.

Below are the most common issues and how you can fix them yourself instead of paying someone else to do it or just throwing the item out.

RETURNING YOUR SHRUNKEN SWEATER TO GROWN-UP SIZE

TOOLBOX

- Baby shampoo, hair conditioner, or fabric softener

THIS IS HOW WE DO IT

As good as your favorite sweater looks on your child's doll, there is a chance you can get it back to its original size. To try to salvage that prized cardi, soak it in water and ¼ cup baby shampoo, hair conditioner, or fabric softener for 20 to 30 minutes, swirling and swishing every few minutes to relax the fibers. Place the sweater on a clean, dry towel and roll it, like a burrito, while gently pressing to absorb some of the excess water. Unroll the sweater and place it on a new dry towel. You now need to slowly pull and stretch it by hand. The goal is to handwork it back into its original size and shape. If needed, you can stuff it (e.g., with towels in the arms). Continue to stretch it if needed until it dries. Just stop when you get the size and shape you want. Remember to work it, slowly pull and stretch it over time.

SEWING ON A BUTTON

TOOLBOX

- Basic sewing kit: spool of thread, thimble, a pair of scissors, and a needle
- The patience of a saint
- Glasses if you wear them (and maybe even if you don't)

THIS IS HOW WE DO IT

1. Cut approximately 24 inches of thread.
2. Slide one end of the thread through the eye of the needle (this usually requires your tongue sticking out to the side while squinting one eye).
3. Pull the thread through the needle until you have equal lengths on both sides with the needle hanging in the

middle. Double-knot the end of the threads. This knot will become the stopper so that the thread won't get pulled through the fabric.

4. Hold the button in place with one hand while pushing the needle up through the back of the fabric and through any one of the holes in the button.

5. Pull the thread all the way until you feel the knot stop against the fabric. Next, for four-hole buttons, push the needle down through the hole that is diagonally across from the hole you just came through (it will look like an x); if it's a two-holer, just go through the other hole.

6. Repeat this two or three times through all of the holes until the button feels secure.

7. To secure and tie off the thread, bring the needle around and through one of the underside loops of thread and pull it tight. Repeat this two to three times.

8. Cut the loose ends of the thread close to the fabric.

SHAVING THE PILLS OFF YOUR CLOTHES

TOOLBOX

- Plug-in fabric shaver (battery-operated is fine, but not my favorite)

THIS IS HOW WE DO IT

Even though I own two already, if I was to get a clothes shaver for a Christmas present, it would make my day. I love them, it's one of the best inventions. Spread out your garment as smooth as you can so that the shaver doesn't get caught on wrinkles, which can cause snags and holes. Gently sweep the shaver back and forth over the surface of the item. Ensure you are emptying the lint catcher as you go; if it gets too full, your shaver will slow down and will not work effectively.

THE PINHOLE PHENOMENON

The mystery has been solved! Ever wondered why every damn T-shirt you own has tiny little holes in the front, usually at the belly button area? Well, let me tell you, it isn't moths. They are common and there are two main causes. The first is by rubbing, because your waist is a primary friction point. Repeated rubbing on your belt, the top of your pants, your buttons, the seat belt, the countertop, the stove (that's a big one), your desk, or even from carrying your kids. To combat this you could get button covers, stop wearing a belt, tuck in your shirt, wear an apron, or just give up and cruise on into a comfy wardrobe consisting entirely of elastic waistband slacks. The second cause is the shirt itself! The reason this typically happens to T-shirts is because retailers/manufacturers of T-shirts choose lower-quality cotton to keep pricing competitive with fast fashion, and these lower-quality knits deteriorate easily with repeated friction.

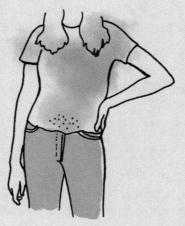

FIXING A BROKEN ZIPPER

TOOLBOX

- Vaseline, soap, or lip balm
- Safety pin, paper clip, or key ring
- Ribbon
- Fork
- Pliers
- Zipper pull replacement
- Pencil

THIS IS HOW WE DO IT

Zippers can (and will) break in multiple ways. These are the most common fixes.

When the Zipper Pull Comes Off

If you need a temporary solution, use a safety pin, key ring, or paper clip.

For a more permanent fix, you can purchase zipper pull replacements or you can use a small piece of material or ribbon threaded through the slider. Just pull it through the slider so that it's exactly halfway through and the ends match in length. Sew a few stitches into the material in the middle and on the end to sew the two ends together. Presto, change-o: new fabric pull!

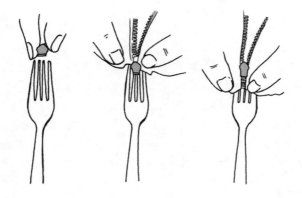

If the slider came off and you still have it, stick it on a fork to hold it in place, narrow side toward the fork. Then just slide the two pins (sides) of the zipper back into the slider and keep pushing until you're back in business.

When the Teeth Split After You've Zipped Them

If your zipper seems to go up fine but then, as soon as it's fastened, all the teeth split or come undone, there is likely an issue with the slider. The function of the slider is to lock the teeth together. Over time, the slider can separate and loosen. To fix, using a pair of pliers, gently and gradually squeeze the top and bottom of the slider in order to bring them closer together. Tightening the slider will stop the teeth from slipping out of the gap.

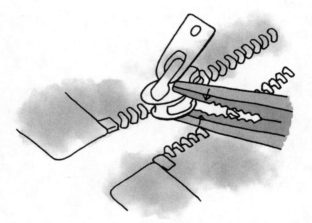

When the Zipper Gets Stuck or Jammed

If the zipper won't move, start by checking to see if there's anything caught in it; even the tiniest thread can prevent it from moving freely. If there is nothing stuck in the teeth or slider, you can try a few things to help it glide. You can use a small amount of soap, Vaseline, or lip balm to lubricate the teeth. We all know lubrication can help with friction. Gently move the pull up and down until it moves freely. Be-

lieve it or not, you can also try using a pencil on the teeth. The graph-
ite in the pencil will also act as a lubricant.

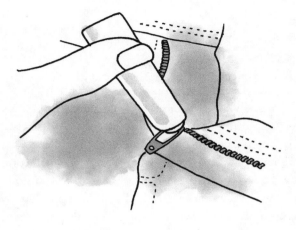

GETTING THE STRING BACK INTO
YOUR HOODIE OR WAISTBAND

TOOLBOX

• Safety pin

THIS IS HOW WE DO IT

This is one of the most annoying and guaranteed-to-happen things.
To get the string back where it came from, attach a safety pin through
one end of the string. Insert the safety pin into one of the openings as
far as you can. Then holding the safety pin with one hand, use your
other hand to scrunch the fabric over the pin so it bunches up. Use
the hand that was bunching to now hold the safety pin while the
other hand pulls the bunched-up fabric away, thus moving the pin
farther along. Repeat until the pin has reached the other opening.
When you've got it through, knot it (make sure the knot is bigger
than the hole it came through) so it doesn't happen again.

ERASING BLEACH STAINS

TOOLBOX

- Sharpies

THIS IS HOW WE DO IT

The term "bleach stain" is a bit misleading because it's not so much a stain as it is an absence of color. My quick and dirty fix is to grab a Sharpie or any other permanent marker and color in the bleached spots. It works best with black (because you don't have to worry about color-matching), but in a pinch, you can get away with other colors, too. I buy the jumbo packs with all the colors. If you don't want to throw away whatever you've bleached and don't feel like dyeing the whole thing, a Sharpie is the best way to touch-up in a pinch.

REMOVING PET HAIR

TOOLBOX

- Vacuum
- Sticky peel-off lint brush; or a roll of packing, masking, or duct tape
- Rubber gloves
- Dryer
- Microfiber
- Pumice stone

THIS IS HOW WE DO IT

The easiest way to remove pet hair is by simply getting rid of your pet, but if you don't want to do that (and I'm guessing you don't), a regular vacuuming is best, however, a simple sticky peel-off lint brush will do for the in-between. I don't like the ones that you can wash—they don't work. You can go ahead and throw those out. Packing, masking, and duct tape work just as effectively if you don't have a sticky roller. Tape is always a great go-to for the hard-to reach spots on your couch—like the tufted holes—or any other nooks and crannies.

Here are some other really good go-tos:

- Rubber gloves: This works best on furniture! Put on your rubber gloves, apply a little pressure and short strokes in one direction to the surface, and wipe your gloved hand over it. The rubber will create friction and the hair will start to come up.
- Microfiber: If you haven't noticed by this point . . . I love these things! A quick hair-removal option is to use a damp microfiber cloth. Similar to the rubber glove, the cloth will create friction when you apply a little pressure and short strokes in one direction to the surface. Simply wipe the cloth and the hair will start to come up.
- Dryer: If the hair is on clothing or blankets, etc., tossing the item in the dryer for a few minutes will help to remove a significant amount of hair before you pull out the lint roller. Even if you are planning to just wash the item, tossing it in the dryer first will help to remove and loosen the hair before the wash.
- Pumice stone: If you have a spot where hair is difficult to remove with a vacuum, try running a pumice stone over the area. The rough texture of a pumice stone helps to lift hair out of carpet and upholstery.

. . .

Just when you feel like throwing in the towel, don't do it . . . it will only make more laundry. Besides, you've already done it. Now you're on your game, caught up and feeling good. Remember when having an empty laundry basket was the best darn thirty seconds of your day . . . well, that's all in the past, you're a regular little keeper-upperer now. In the same way washing machines have come a long way since my nan's wringer, so have you.

WE'VE REACHED THE END. Recap:

- If you like your clothes the color they are now, always sort your laundry.
- Don't stick your finger in a wringer—it hurts.
- Keep up instead of catching up. (Maybe the more times I say it, the more it will sink in.)
- For the love of God, please stop using fabric softener and dryer sheets.
- More scent doesn't mean more clean.
- I love balls . . . in my dryer.
- Bluing . . . nothing to do with balls, get your mind out of the gutter, is a great way to get your whites whiter.
- A night of stripping can have a big payoff.

3.

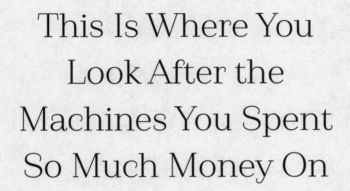

This Is Where You Look After the Machines You Spent So Much Money On

DISHWASHERS

This Is Where You Realize the Machine Actually Does Clean Your Dishes the First Time When You Use It Properly

. . .

S O, HERE'S SOMETHING I HINTED AT EARLIER AND SAVED until the end because first I wanted to make you realize that you can do more than you ever thought you could, before I broke this news to you: The machines in your home also need TLC. I know. It's a drag. The whole point of a machine is that it's supposed to do all of the work, right? But in order to do the work, those machines need care. Just like any relationship in your life, if you neglect it, it's probably not going to be there for you when you need it. Routine maintenance of your machines will save you a lot of headaches (and money) later on, because it'll keep them working properly and lengthen their life cycle.

The difference between cleaning and maintaining your machines and appliances is the difference between washing your car and getting the oil changed. If you go a long time without washing your car, it might not look pretty, but it'll still run. But wait too long to change the oil and eventually your car won't start. Every machine in your house needs some sort of care or maintenance. These are the ones that need the most love and attention (so needy).

TOOLBOX

- Rinse aid
- Distilled white vinegar
- Bowl, mug, or glass measuring cup
- Skewers or toothpicks
- Baking soda
- Dishwasher cleaning tabs

THIS IS HOW WE DO IT

(I hope you are now also dancing in addition to singing.)

Be a Low-Key Rinser

There are typically two kinds of people when it comes to dishwasher loaders: those who want to be able to throw in their super-dirty dishes and have them come out immaculate, and those who insist on rinsing and scrubbing everything before it goes into the machine (thereby eliminating the point of the machine). Here's a secret: The key is to scrape off anything larger than a grain of rice. That's it! There is no need to rinse. The dishwasher detergent needs a job to do and that is to cling to food particles and break them down. Without a job to do, the detergent will cling to the dishes and the machine itself, causing residue, and you may feel like you can taste the detergent during your next meal. During the pre-wash, soil sensors detect the amount of soil in the water which determines the intensity of the cycle.

Don't Crowd Your Dishes

Same premise as with laundry: Water and detergent need space to do their job. If there is something blocking or stopping the spray arm from spinning, the water will not be able to dissolve the detergent or reach all of the dishes. This will prevent your dishes from getting clean. If you are someone who considers it a victory if there is not one bit of empty space in the machine and you managed to fit every single dish, glass, and fork from your dinner party for twelve into one load, you are not doing your machine or your stemware any favors. Your machine can't work effectively and nothing will get clean. Piling up and overlapping your dishes is like showering with your clothes on.

Do Not Put Cups over the Tines

Your dishwasher was designed to hold your cups, mugs, and glasses off to the side of the rack at an angle. The angle is to allow the water to run off of them. If they're balancing on a tine (the upright stems in your dishwasher), they could rattle around and break.

Don't Buy Dishwasher Detergent in Bulk

Dishwasher detergent doesn't "go bad" but its effectiveness is reduced over time. As tempting as it is, refrain from buying more detergent than you can use within 3 to 4 months. Some can last longer than others but over time their performance can start to diminish.

Never Use Dish Soap in Your Machine

Dish soap is way too thick and sudsy for the dishwasher. It was designed to be used in a sink for washing dishes by hand. If you're out of dishwasher detergent, it might be tempting to use dish soap, but your machine can't take it.

Skip the Foil

Putting a piece of balled-up aluminum foil in your cutlery basket . . . will do nothing! It won't reduce water marks or make your glasses sparkle. As for shining, removing scratches or rust from cutlery, it's not really doing much for that either. The cutlery (each piece) would need to be in direct contact with the foil for any reaction to occur.

Alternate Up and Down for Cutlery
If You Don't Have a Cover

If your cutlery basket has cell covers, use them! It's to keep everything separate. Otherwise, just alternate them up and down, except for knives, which should always go down for safety. Don't let your spoons spoon.

Know Who Is a Top and Who Is a Bottom

Soup bowls, cups, glasses, mugs, large utensils, and plastic go on the top. Plates, pots and pans, large dishes, and large bowls go on the bottom.

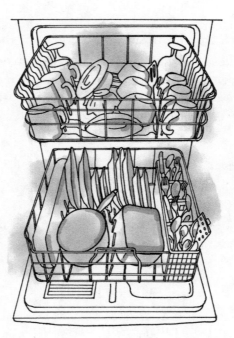

Started from the Bottom, Now We're Here

When unloading your dishwasher, start with the bottom rack first. That way the water from the dishes on the top rack won't drip onto the dishes on the bottom. Believe me, it's simple but this is a game changer!

Make Sure the Detergent Door Isn't Gummed Up

Always put your detergent in the compartment. If you're putting your detergent in the bottom of the machine, it will be rinsed away in the pre-wash cycle, leaving the main cycle to wash your dishes with water alone. During pre-wash, that water is drained and new water is pumped in; it is at this point that the compartment door is opened and the detergent is dispensed. If the reason you are putting the detergent in the bottom of the machine is because the compartment door isn't functioning properly, here are a few of the main fixes. If the compartment door is gummed up, it will be unable to open and release the detergent. So make sure that it is kept clean. Large items blocking the compartment door can also interfere with its ability to open. Wet hands or a wet compartment can cause the water-activated film on the pod/tab to partially dissolve, sticking it to the compartment and not releasing.

Rinse Aid . . . It's in the Name, It Helps

A rinse aid agent isn't just a gimmick or bougie extra for the elite dishwashing crowd (does that exist?). Your machine is designed to function best with it. That compartment is real: Rinse aid lowers the surface tension of the water so it slides/sheets right off of the dishes, preventing water spots. It helps to dry your dishes faster and more effectively. Most manufacturers recommend it for the best results, and so do I!

Your Filter Won't Clean Itself

You need to clean your dishwasher so your dishwasher can clean your dishes. If you have a smelly dishwasher, the most common problem is usually the filter. Check often to make sure the filter is free from food, bones, wrappers, stickers, hair (don't ask), and who knows what else.

Otherwise the food and yuck will eventually just make its way back onto the dishes during the cycle. Once a week (depending on use), pop that sucker out and give it a good rinse. All dishwashers have a filter. Older models may have an automatic filter that grinds up food particles and washes them away with the wastewater, but much more common is the manual filter. You will need to remove it and clean it regularly, even if you don't use your dishwasher daily. The filter should be a pop-out or a twist-out, usually a small basket located in the bottom of the dishwasher. You can access it easily by either pulling out the bottom rack or removing the rack all together. It only needs a wash and rinse with some Dawn and water. Once it's all clean, pop it back in. A dirty filter won't damage your dishwasher, but it will definitely affect its performance and your gag reflex. It's a good idea to leave the dishwasher door slightly ajar (just a crack) when it's not in use. This will allow the dishwasher to completely dry between cycles and air out.

Clean the Inside of Your Machine Regularly

I hate to break it to you, but dishwasher maintenance doesn't stop at cleaning the filter. Once a month your dishwasher needs a deep clean, here's how.

1. Start with cleaning your filter (see above).
2. Wipe the areas around and under the filter (once it's out) with some distilled white vinegar.
3. Wipe the rubber seals on the door.
4. Wipe down the detergent compartment.
5. Spray the entire interior of the dishwasher—top, bottom, sides, soap dispenser—with vinegar and let sit for about 30 minutes. (That'll break down all of the hard water.)
6. Use a skewer or toothpick to clean out the holes in the spray arms. Hard water can jam up the holes and make the water come out all sputtery.
7. Pour vinegar into a bowl, mug, or glass measuring cup and place it upright on the top rack and run on the hottest/longest cycle.

8. Sprinkle some baking soda in the bottom of the machine and run another cycle.

9. An alternative to the above is to purchase and use a dishwasher cleaning tab.

Know When It's Time to Call a Professional

This might sound like it runs counter to everything I've said up until this point, but it's important and it applies to every single appliance in this section, not just dishwashers: You can't do everything yourself. There's a reason professionals exist, and dishwashers are one of the prime examples of an appliance that often needs an expert touch. If no matter what you do you cannot get the water to drain or the dishes will not get clean, you may need to call in a professional.

WASHERS AND DRYERS

This Is Where You Find Out That Your Machines Have More Options Than Stop and Start

. . .

TOOLBOX

- Bleach
- Baking soda
- Straw brush (the one that came with your eco reusable straws)
- Towel
- Cloths
- Vacuum
- Washing machine cleaning tabs
- Brush
- Flexible lint-removing brush
- Rubbing alcohol

First, let's get to know our washing machines, shall we?

Top-Loaders vs. Front-Loaders

Top-Loader Pros

- Familiarity

If you feel like a flip-phone person in a smartphone world, a top-loader may be just the thing for you. They're what most

Front loader   Top loader

people had in their homes growing up, and approximately 70 percent of households still do.

• No lock feature
Ever started a load of laundry and then realized that you forgot that one stray sock or pillowcase? The infamous "midcycle add" is a million times easier with a top-loader because the door doesn't lock, and you can just open that baby up. With front-loaders, the door locks to keep water from leaking out, so if you need to add something midcycle, you have to hit pause or stop the entire cycle and restart it again.

• Cost
Top-loaders are generally cheaper than front-loaders to buy and maintain.

• Ergonomics
For anyone who values comfort and ease, it's simply more comfortable to load and unload from the top of the washer than it is from below. There is little to no bending required.

• Maintenance
Top-loaders require only basic cleaning compared to a front-loader.

Top-Loader Cons

- Energy costs

Top-loaders use more water than front-loaders and require more energy to heat all that water.

- Stacking

Top-load washers need a minimum amount of space for lid clearance, so this limits your ability to take advantage of vertical space by stacking your washer and dryer.

- Ergonomics

Yes, it's a pro and a con. Shorter users may have difficulty reaching the bottom of the drum.

Front-Loader Pros

- Energy costs

Front-loaders use much less water per load than top-loaders and require less energy, which is better for the environment.

- Speed

Front-loaders spin much faster than top-loaders; they are the motorcycle to the top-loader's bicycle. Faster spin means your clothes will come out drier, which means they will need less drying time. Less drying time means less energy used.

- Capacity

Although there are some top-loaders with large capacity, front-loaders generally have bigger drums, meaning more capacity.

- Options

For those who love fancy options like auto detergent dispensers and fabric care features like steam, front-loaders may be for you.

Front-Loader Cons

- Maintenance

Front-loaders can develop a funky smell. That's because
moisture gets trapped in the gaskets (or rubber seals) around
the door, leading to mold and odor. Cleaning and keeping it
dry is essential. It may have a removable filter that requires
cleaning.

- Ergonomics

For anyone who values comfort and ease, it's just more
comfortable to load and unload laundry from the top of
the washer. There is a considerable amount of bending required with a front-loader, even if the machine is on a
stand.

- Aesthetics

The door needs to be kept open at all times when not in use
to prevent moisture from getting trapped and causing mold
and odor. Aesthetically and for space (laundry closet), you
may not love that.

Fun fact: The Samsung front-loader will delight you with a melody from Franz Schubert's *Piano Quintet in A Major,* also known as
the *Trout Quintet*. And the LG plays a melody loosely based on the
English folk tune "The Lincolnshire Poacher."

THIS IS HOW WE DO IT

For Front-Loading Washers

Once a week you should run the tub clean cycle on your front-loader
(most machines have one) with no detergent. Once a month you
should do a deep clean of your machine.

- All detergent drawers can be removed; there will be a release latch, and this is much easier to get into all those nooks and crannies. Simply wash it with soap and water, dry it, and pop it back in the machine.
- To clean and deodorize the inside of the drum, sprinkle some baking soda and water and wipe down the entire drum.
- Filters can be a little hard to find (sometimes located on front, side, or back of machine; see your individual model manual). Before opening the trap door covering the filter, lay a towel down under and in front, as water will come out during this process. Open the trap door. If you see a small hose, gently pull it from its clip, remove the cap, and drain the water. You can use a straw brush to clean out the hose. Turn the filter to the left and pull out. Rinse it in a sink with soap and water and put it back. Replace the cap onto the hose and put it back into its clip.
- To clean the rubber gasket, you can use one of two methods, depending on the condition of your gasket. If you have mold or mildew, a mixture of bleach and water will be the most effective. If there are no obvious signs of mold and mildew, you can opt for a baking soda and water mixture. Whichever method you choose, use a cleaning brush and a cloth to scrub the gasket, making sure to thoroughly clean all areas of the gasket.
- Follow this by adding 2 cups of distilled white vinegar to the detergent dispenser and run a tub clean cycle. To deodorize, add 1 cup of baking soda and run the tub clean once more.
- An alternative to the above is to purchase and use a commercial washing machine cleaning tab.

For Top-Loading Washers

With a top-loader, you don't have to worry about moldy, smelly gaskets. Once a week wipe down the controls, lid (inside and outside), lid switch, and the detergent/fabric softener compartments, to keep your machine in good shape. Once a month you should do a deep clean of your machine. Here are two options depending on your cleaning product of choice.

Option 1: Bleach

1. Wipe out the compartments with a wet cloth.
2. Start a wash cycle (without detergent) on hot.
3. Pour 1 cup of bleach into the drum and about ¼ cup of bleach into both the detergent and fabric softener compartments.
4. Close the lid, then run the machine for about 1 minute to mix the bleach and water.
5. Open the machine lid and let sit for about 30 minutes.
6. Close the lid and let the machine run a full cycle.
7. Directly after, you should run another full cycle, with no products, to make sure the bleach has fully cleared.

Option 2: Baking Soda

1. Wipe out the compartments with a wet cloth.
2. Sprinkle baking soda in and around the drum. Spritz a little water and give it a little wipe with a cloth.
3. Start a wash cycle (without detergent) on hot.
4. Close the lid, then run the machine for about 1 minute to mix the baking soda and water.
5. Open the machine lid and let sit for at least 15 minutes.
6. Close the lid and let the machine run a full cycle.

Dealing with the Dryer

Once a month, wipe down the inside and the outside of the dryer. Use rubbing alcohol to clean the sensors on the inside of the dryer. Vacuum behind and underneath the dryer as dirt and lint can accumulate quickly.

Lint should be removed before or after every load. Yes, every load! Pull out the lint screen, every machine is different, and remove the lint. Having a lint container or garbage nearby is a good reminder. I like to keep a cute magnetic lint holder on the side of my machine. Some of the lint will get past the lint screen and remain in the cavity of the dryer. Every 3 months it's a good idea to remove the lint screen and vacuum within that cavity as far as your vacuum attachment will reach. You can also purchase a flexible lint removal brush to remove the lint by hand from this cavity.

Dryer safety should be taken seriously. Unmaintained dryers can pose a fire risk for your home. A good rule of thumb is to have your dryer exhaust vents inspected and cleaned by a professional at least once a year.

ANYTHING ELSE
WITH A FILTER

This Is Where You Stop Lying About How Often You Change Your Filter and Actually Start Doing It

. . .

TOOLBOX

- Dawn or degreaser
- Distilled white vinegar
- Cup or container
- Toothbrush
- Sponge or cloth
- Filters (of course)
- Vacuum or brush

THIS IS HOW WE DO IT

Filter . . . What Filter?

Any machine or appliance in your home that uses water, circulates air, etc., will almost always have a filter. I hate to break it to you, but these filters will need to be changed or cleaned regularly to keep your machine working properly. For every machine it's best to read your manual and follow the guidelines for recommendations on cleaning and changing schedules. There are so many variables among machines and models that I can't say with 100 percent certainty what you should specifically do without getting the manual involved. My point is you may have a machine that also has its own set of specific instructions, so follow mine as a general guide but always, *always,* read and follow the manufacturer's instruction manual. I recommend keeping track of your filter-changing schedule in your calendar.

A Lot of Your Filters Are Washable

Meaning, when it's time to change a filter, you don't necessarily need to run out and replace it. I'll get more specific about what kind of filters can be washed and which should be replaced.

Reservoirs Aren't Filters

Some small appliances (like clothing steamers, single-serve coffee makers, humidifiers, and CPAP machines) have reservoirs that hold a small amount of water in a tank to operate. This water may need to be changed every use or every few uses. I know what you're thinking: But the water heats up! Doesn't that . . . neutralize all the bad things? The answer is not really. If water is left sitting in your appliances for long periods of time, minerals can build up, ultimately causing operating issues. This is particularly true if you have hard water. Think about it like this: If you poured a glass of water today and left it on the counter, would you drink it in 6 months? Probably not. Your appliances need clean fresh water. Distilled water is best for use in health-related equipment like CPAP machines and humidifiers.

Consider Filter Maintenance
Before You Buy

Do your filter research before you buy. If something has a filter that costs $70 to change every month, or if it's hard to find, it may not be the appliance for you. Think of it this way: If your kid wanted a toy that required 40 AAA batteries, would that stop you from buying it?

There's no right answer, there's just knowing yourself and making decisions based on your wants and needs. Four good questions to ask yourself about any appliance that features a filter are:

- Is it washable or replaceable?
- Where can I get it?
- Can I easily get it?
- How much is it?

Here are some things in your home with filters that need to be cleaned and/or replaced:

Humidifiers and Dehumidifiers

Which machine does what? In general, humidifiers:
- add moisture to dry air (like in winter)
- help with nasal and sinus congestion in cold weather
- helps with dry itchy eyes, dry skin, and chapped lips
- stave off cracks and shrinking in wood, plaster, and leather furniture

Meanwhile, dehumidifiers:
- remove moisture from the air (typically in spring and summer)
- make the house feel less sticky and damp
- reduce moisture and humidity, which can cause mold
- fight carpenter ants, wood beetles, and termites, which are attracted to moisture

Both are only as effective as their filters are clean. Most humidifiers have a filter that removes particles and bacteria from water before it is pushed into the air. You will need to change the filter regularly in order to keep the air clean and your humidifier in good condition. The frequency of changing the filter will depend on the quality of your water supply and how often you are using the humidifier. Dehumidifiers, on the other hand, typically have filters that can be washed rather than replaced, which is a great money saver. In terms of frequency, most machines have an indicator sound/light that tells you when you need to change or wash it.

Faucet Screen Filter (Aerator)

Did you know that your kitchen and bathroom faucets have a mini filter? It's actually an important part of the faucet. Faucet screens or aerators are there to filter and aerate the water while ensuring water does not spray everywhere. Take a look and you'll see that your faucet may have a tiny screen. If you have noticed that your water stream has slowed, it may be time to clean the faucet screen or install a new one. Over time, faucet aerator screens can get clogged from the minerals in tap water. (If you're regularly soaking your faucets in bags of vinegar—see Hacking Away at Hard Water, page 67—you likely won't need to do this.) Faucet screens can be cleaned as often as once per week or as little as once per year. To clean:

1. If you have a removable aerator, twist it off and take it apart (making mental notes or *actual* notes as you go so you know how to put it back together).

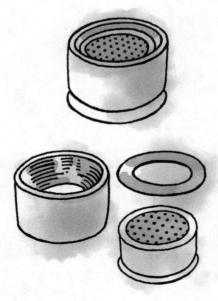

2. Place the pieces in a cup or container of distilled white vinegar to soak for a few minutes. Then, remove them to scrub with a toothbrush.

3. Finally, rinse thoroughly, reassemble, and thread the aerator back on the faucet.

Coffee Maker

This life-saving device may have a filter. If it does have a filter, it should be replaced as required. First, for clarity, I am not talking about the paper filters you put into a drip coffee machine, I'm talking about the filter that more modern single-use coffee makers have. Some are optional but their function is to absorb pollutants and to remove debris from the water in order to keep them from getting into your cup. Once the filters are full, they no longer work and will need to be replaced. Again, you should stick to the specific machine's recommendations. It's usually about every 3 months. Additionally, any coffee maker with a water reservoir needs to be cleaned, descaled, and disinfected regularly in order to run trouble-free while producing a good cup of joe!

If you have hard water, you may need to descale the machine and change the filter more often.

Changing your filter can be a good prompt to give your coffee machine a deep clean and descale. Simply remove the filter and fill the reservoir halfway with white vinegar and the rest with plain water. Allow it to run through several brewing cycles without a pod until the reservoir is empty. Repeat with plain water and replace the filter. For a drip coffee maker, add 2 to 4 cups white vinegar and allow it to run through a brewing cycle without coffee. Repeat with plain water until the vinegar smell is gone. Some manufacturers will recommend specific descaling solutions or tablets.

Window AC Unit

All window AC units have a filter that should be checked and cleaned at least once per month during heavy-use periods. A clean filter is absolutely crucial to properly cool your home with fewer impurities.

Just remove the filter and vacuum or brush it to remove any heavy dirt and dust, then soak it in Dawn and water. Allow it to air-dry and put it back in the unit.

Vacuum Cleaner

Failing to change or clean the filters in your vacuum cleaner could cause it to lose suction or blow excessive dust back into the air. Changing or cleaning the filters regularly will save your vacuum and air quality. Each model is different, so refer to the manufacturer's instruction manual to see how often the filter should be changed or cleaned. Pro tip: Because air comes out of the vacuum while you use it, putting some cinnamon or scent beads in the vacuum bag or canister will make the house smell great.

Refrigerator

If you have a water dispenser or an icemaker in your refrigerator, you have a filter that removes the small particles and impurities that cause bad taste and odor. The filters need to be replaced according to the guidelines in your owner's manual, generally every 6 months.

Hair Dryer

Did you know it had a filter? Did you know that you should be cleaning it regularly? Like any other electric appliance, it requires maintenance, usually around once a month depending on how often you use it. Regardless of whether you have invested in a high-end hair dryer or drugstore special, if you aren't properly maintaining it, it will stop working at some point. A hot, dirty, and clogged hair dryer can be a hazard. The filter can become blocked with hair, dust, dirt, and hair sprays. A clogged dryer filter will prevent air from being pushed out, and the internal temperature of the hair dryer can end up becoming too high. When not enough air can get through the filter, your hair will take longer to dry. So those are all the reasons to clean your dryer filter, now here's how:

- Simply remove the filter located on the back of the dryer. Some twist or pull off, others may require a screwdriver.

- Brush, wipe, or vacuum off the debris and place the filter under running water until it's clean.
- Ensure that it is completely dry before reattaching it.

Range Hoods

- Range hoods have grease filters that should be checked and cleaned once a month, or more often if you cook frequently. They should be replaced every 1 to 2 years depending on use.

If you have a ductless range hood (it doesn't vent to the outside of your home), in addition to your grease filter, you will also have a charcoal filter. A charcoal filter cannot be cleaned; it will have to be replaced as needed or recommended. The grease filter is usually an aluminum mesh removeable rectangular filter. The aluminum material catches grease while the charcoal neutralizes odors and particles. A filter with grease buildup will not allow the fan to properly filter or exhaust cooking fumes and heat, which will cause a greasy, sticky film on appliances, walls, and ceilings. To remove, clean and reinstall these:

1. Slide out the grease filters from the hood.
2. Soak them in a sink filled with hot water and Dawn for 20 minutes.
3. Carefully remove any remaining grease or debris with a sponge or cloth.
4. Allow them to air-dry and reinstall.
5. Alternatively, you can wash grease filters in the dishwasher or use a degreaser.

Over-the-Range Microwave

- Similar to a range hood's, these filters also need to be checked and cleaned once a month, or more often if you cook frequently. They should be replaced every 1 to 2 years depending on use.

(If you have a countertop microwave, there's no filter.) If your microwave doesn't vent to the outside of your home, it will have both a grease filter and a charcoal filter (which cannot be cleaned and must be replaced). The charcoal filter absorbs odors from cooking. You should replace your charcoal filter about every 6 months. A filter with grease buildup will not allow the fan to properly filter or exhaust cooking fumes and heat. This will cause a greasy, sticky film on appliances, walls, and ceilings. To remove, clean, and reinstall these:

1. Slide the grease filters out of the microwave.
2. Soak them in a sink filled with hot water and Dawn for 20 minutes.
3. Carefully remove any remaining grease or debris with a sponge or cloth.
4. Allow them to air-dry and reinstall.
5. Alternatively, you can wash grease filters in the dishwasher or use a degreaser.

Gas Furnace

If you have a gas furnace (if you pay a gas bill, you do), it has a filter, and if you are not maintaining that filter on a regular basis, you could end up with poor air quality, a breakdown, higher bills, and a less efficient machine. A dirty filter forces the furnace to work harder. Furnace filters reduce particle buildup inside your furnace, keeping the indoor air as clean as possible. You should be regularly checking your furnace filter but the best practice is to change it every 3 months. You may need to change your filter more often if you're undergoing renovations, if you have pets, if you have anyone in the home with asthma or allergies, or if your furnace gets heavy use. Pull out your filter and hold it up to the light. If you can't easily see the light through the filter, it's time to switch it out. Filters will vary, from washable to disposable to HEPA filters in areas with poor-quality air. Replace with the correct filter and size for your furnace according to the manufacturer's recommendations.

Air Purifier

Most air purifiers have a change filter indicator (often a light) that alerts you when the filter should be replaced. The main filter should be replaced about every 6 months, or according to the owner's manual.

Window Screens

These are just big filters between your home and the outside world! Check your window screens regularly for dirt, tears, or "the saggies." To clean them:

- Remove the screen from the window.
- Gently spray with a low-pressure hose (outdoors) or shower-head (inside).
- Use some Dawn on a soft brush to remove dirt if needed.
- Allow to air-dry.
- If your screen is torn or ripped, you can actually sew it to-gether with a needle and thread or patch it.
- If there are large tears or if the screen is overly loose or saggy, you may consider replacing it.

. . .

You know this next part. RECAP!
- Maintain the machines you spent a fortune on.
- Load your dishwasher the way I told you to (I don't want to fight about this; put your knives down—literally, in the dish-washer, down).
- Keep the door open on your front-loading washing machine, even if it looks ugly.
- Whatever appliance you're staring at probably has a filter; look for it and change/clean it.

SO THERE YOU GO,
NOW YOU KNOW

. . .

CAN YOU BELIEVE YOU JUST READ A BOOK ABOUT CLEANING and laundry? I can't believe I just wrote one. I'm sure my nan would be proud. But let's face it, the real winner of this book is Montell Jordan, because without his '90s hit we wouldn't know that "This Is How We Do It."

What I'm most proud of is you. You read this book because you wanted to make a change and that's the first step. I'm proud of you if you read this book because you needed help with these things. It's not easy asking for help, especially about things other people seem to just know instinctively. I'm proud of you if you already were a cleaning pro and just wanted some more tips and tricks; good on you. I'm also proud of you if you just read this book for the caulk and ball jokes, you dirty bitch. Whatever the reason, I hope you got something out of it. I hope it helped with the overwhelming feelings that cleaning, laundry, and maintenance often bring. Even if you take away just one thing that makes your life a little bit easier or a hack that you can flex about to your friends that you now know and they don't, that would make me happy.

When I first started writing this book about cleaning, laundry, and maintenance I thought long and hard about what those things do for me. Why do I do it and why is it important to me? And the answer was self-care. Self-care isn't just about spa treatments, yoga, and meditation; it isn't selfish or extravagant. Self-care is important because it helps us maintain balance in our lives. For me, it's keeping a tidy and organized home, the routine of laundry, and the confidence that comes from doing my own home maintenance. Think of self-care as a full tank of gas: Without it, you'll be running on empty, unable to keep up. This idea of keep-up instead of catch-up really is something that saves me in life.

When people feel stress, anxiety, guilt, and shame about housework, it's because they don't think about the big picture, the end result. The end result actually brings about the exact opposite feelings; it brings feelings of peace, calmness, accomplishment, and empowerment. When I am caught up with my day-to-day tasks, I think of how good it makes me feel and how much time I have afforded myself to do the things I love, with the people I love. It was the reason I wrote this book, and it's the message I want you to take away from it.

ACKNOWLEDGMENTS

. . .

To my nan, who taught me so much about so much.

To my mother, who I wish more than anything could have read this book.

To my dad, for always accepting my teenage collect calls when I didn't have a quarter. For supporting me in everything I have ever done. For the endless hours of volunteering, coaching, and taxiing me to every sporting practice and event.

To my sisters, for raising me after Mom and Dad gave up on it. You're welcome for me never telling on you for having boys over, smoking cigarettes, and telling me it was fine to eat the entire bottle of Flintstones vitamins on Christmas morning.

I would like to acknowledge the shocking audacity of the lady who spanked me in the parking garage for shooting a cap gun when I was eight.

To my best and only friend, Michelle, for loving and supporting my attention span, my brief crime-scene sketching career, my lack of note-taking, but most of all for remembering all of my passwords. And to Fred (our shared husband), for all of the beautiful hugs that Michelle and her cold heart have no interest in.

To Trace again, because I want to thank you for loving me the way you do. We have somehow managed to make this work even if we did move in together on our first date. I knew from the moment I saw your face that I loved you.

To the people who invented the Animator toy in the '80s. This toy was a huge disappointment. I had so many high hopes for this hand-held technology, which were all crushed that Christmas morning.

To my online community . . . without you I would be washing and folding alone . . . without music, without winks, without pats; just wash, fold, and repeat.

To Carla, for all of your hard work, enthusiasm, long phone calls, and patience.

To Dan, for tracking me down and getting the ball rolling.

A special thanks to Katy Nishimoto, Whitney Frick, Rose Fox, Avideh Bashirrad, and the rest of the Dial family.

Thank you to the pandemic and to HannahBreadTok, for without the two of you, none of this would have been possible.

ABOUT THE AUTHOR

In addition to creating viral videos with
housecleaning tips and tricks, MELISSA DILKES PATERAS
has worked in social services for more than twenty years,
specializing in behavior and relationship management.
She lives in Ontario, Canada, with her wife and three children.

TikTok: @melissadilkespateras
Instagram: @melissadilkespateras
Facebook.com/melissa.d.pateras

ABOUT THE TYPE

This book was set in Caslon, a typeface first
designed in 1722 by William Caslon (1692–1766).
Its widespread use by most English printers in the
early eighteenth century soon supplanted the Dutch
typefaces that had formerly prevailed. The roman is
considered a "workhorse" typeface due to its pleasant,
open appearance, while the italic is
exceedingly decorative.

The Dial Press, an imprint of Random House,
publishes books driven by the heart.

Follow us on Instagram:
@THEDIALPRESS

Discover other Dial Press books and
sign up for our e-newsletter:

thedialpress.com

Your personal information will be processed in
accordance with our privacy policy, located here:
penguinrandomhouse.com/privacy